Quick and Easy, Proven Recipes

Perfect Pasta

D1736689

Publisher's Note: Raw or semi-cooked eggs should not be consumed by babies, toddlers, pregnant or breastfeeding women, the elderly or those suffering from a chronic illness.

Publisher & Creative Director: Nick Wells
Project Editor: Catherine Taylor
Art Director: Mike Spender
Layout Design: Jane Ashley
Digital Design & Production: Chris Herbert

Special thanks to Emma Chafer and Esme Chapman.

This is a **FLAME TREE** Book

FLAME TREE PUBLISHING
Crabtree Hall, Crabtree Lane
Fulham, London SW6 6TY
United Kingdom
www.flametreepublishing.com

First published 2014

Copyright © 2014 Flame Tree Publishing Ltd

14 16 18 17 15
1 3 5 4 2

ISBN: 978-1-78361-224-6

Printed in Singapore

All images © Flame Tree Publishing Ltd, except for the following which are © **Shutterstock.com** and the following contributors: Brittny 8; Christian Jung 9; cretolamna 10bl; Olesya Feketa 10tl; Lisovskaya Natalia 11; schankz 12; bitt24 13tr; Netfalls-Remy Musser 13br; Lapina Maria 14; Jill Chen 15; Olga Nayashkova 16; Nils Z 17; kuvona 18; draconus 19; Natalila Pyzhova 20; DenisNata 21; tinnko 22; Galina Mikhalishina 23; Robyn Mackenzie 24; Hong Vo 25; gosphotodesign 26; marilyn barbone 27; Mariontxa 28; Ramon L. Farinos 29; Somchai Som 30; Boiarkina Marina 31tr; Denisa V 31br; Bernd Schmidt 32tl; Monkey Business Images 32bl; nexus 7 33; Only Fabrizio 34; Volosina 35; Maxal Tamor 36; brulove 37.

Quick and Easy, Proven Recipes

Perfect Pasta

**FLAME TREE
PUBLISHING**

Contents

Essentials

With practical information on everything from choosing the best pasta shapes to how to cook perfect pasta and what wine to serve with your meal, this chapter is a great way to kick-start your passion for pasta. With must know information on basic hygiene practices you will be able to cook and keep calm in your kitchen.

Hygiene in the Kitchen

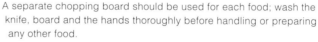

It is well worth remembering that many foods can carry some form of bacteria. In most cases, the worst it will lead to is a bout of food poisoning or gastroenteritis, although for certain people this can be more serious. The risk can be reduced or eliminated by good food hygiene and proper cooking.

Do not buy food that is past its sell-by date and do not consume any food that is past its use-by date. When buying food, use your eyes and nose. If the food looks tired, limp or a bad colour or it has a rank, acrid or simply bad smell, do not buy or eat it under any circumstances. Do take special care when preparing raw meat and fish.

A separate chopping board should be used for each food; wash the knife, board and the hands thoroughly before handling or preparing any other food.

Regularly clean, defrost and clear out the refrigerator or freezer – it is worth checking the packaging to see exactly how long each product is safe to freeze.

Avoid handling food if suffering from an upset stomach, as bacteria can be passed on through food preparation.

Dish cloths and tea towels must be washed and changed regularly. Ideally, use disposable cloths, which should be replaced on a daily basis. More durable cloths should be left to soak in bleach, then washed in the washing machine on a boil wash.

Keep hands, cooking utensils and food preparation surfaces clean and do not allow pets to climb onto any work surfaces.

Buying

Avoid bulk buying where possible, especially fresh produce such as meat, poultry, fish, fruit and vegetables, unless buying for the freezer. Fresh foods lose their nutritional value rapidly, so buying a little at a time minimises loss of nutrients. It also eliminates a packed refrigerator, which reduces the effectiveness of the refrigeration process.

When buying prepackaged goods such as cans or pots of cream and yogurts, check that the packaging is intact and not damaged or pierced at all. Cans should not be dented, pierced or rusty. Check the sell-by dates even for cans and packets of dry ingredients such as flour and rice. Store fresh foods in the refrigerator as soon as possible – not in the car or the office.

When buying frozen foods, ensure that they are not heavily iced on the outside and the contents feel completely frozen. Ensure that the frozen foods have been stored in the cabinet at the correct storage level and the temperature is below -18°C/-0.4°F. Pack in cool bags to transport home and place in the freezer as soon as possible after purchase.

Preparation

Make sure that all work surfaces and utensils are clean and dry. Hygiene should be given priority at all times. Separate chopping boards should be used for raw and cooked meats, fish and vegetables. Currently, a variety of good-quality plastic boards come in various designs and colours. This makes differentiating easier and the plastic has the added hygienic

Hygiene in the Kitchen

advantage of being washable at high temperatures in the dishwasher. (NB: If using the board for fish, first wash in cold water, then in hot, to prevent odour!) Also, remember that knives and utensils should always be thoroughly cleaned after use.

When cooking, be particularly careful to keep cooked and raw food separate to avoid any contamination. It is worth washing all fruits and vegetables, regardless of whether they are going to be eaten raw or lightly cooked. This rule should apply even to prewashed herbs and salads.

Do not reheat food more than once. If using a microwave, always check that the food is piping hot all the way through. In theory, the food should reach a minimum temperature of 70°C/158°F and needs to be cooked at that temperature for at least 3 minutes to ensure that any bacteria in the food are killed.

All poultry must be thoroughly thawed before using, including chicken and poussin. Remove the food to be thawed from the freezer and place in a shallow dish to contain the juices.

Leave the food in the refrigerator until it is completely thawed. A 1.4 kg/3 lb whole chicken will take about 26–30 hours to thaw. To speed up the process, immerse the chicken in cold water. However, make sure that the water is changed regularly. When the joints can move freely and no ice crystals remain in the cavity, the bird is completely thawed.

Once thawed, remove the wrapper and pat the chicken dry. Place the chicken in a shallow dish, cover lightly and if storing, store as close to the base of the refrigerator as possible. The chicken should be cooked as soon as possible.

Some foods can be cooked from frozen, including many prepacked foods such as soups, sauces, casseroles and breads. Where applicable, follow the manufacturers' instructions.

Vegetables and fruits can also be cooked from frozen, but meats and fish should be thawed first. The only time food can be refrozen is when the food has been thoroughly thawed, then cooked. Once the food has cooled, then it can be frozen again. On such occasions, the food can only be stored for one month.

All poultry and game (except for duck) must be cooked thoroughly. When cooked, the juices will run clear from the thickest part of the bird – the best area to try is usually the thigh. Other meats, such as minced meat and pork, should be cooked right the way through. Fish should turn opaque, be firm in texture and break easily into large flakes.

When cooking leftovers, make sure they are reheated until piping hot and that any sauce or soup reaches boiling point first before eating.

Storing, Refrigerating and Freezing

Meat, poultry, fish, seafood and dairy products should all be refrigerated. The temperature of the refrigerator should be between 1–5°C/34–41°F, while the freezer temperature should not rise above -18°C/-0.4°F.

To ensure the optimum refrigerator and freezer temperature, avoid leaving the door open for a long time. Try not to overstock the refrigerator, as this reduces the airflow inside and affects the

Hygiene in the Kitchen

efficiency in cooling the food within. When refrigerating cooked food, allow it to cool down quickly and completely before refrigerating. Hot food will raise the temperature of the refrigerator and possibly affect or spoil other food stored in it.

Food within the refrigerator and freezer should always be covered. Raw and cooked food should be stored in separate parts of the refrigerator. Cooked food should be kept on the top shelves of the refrigerator, while raw meat, poultry and fish should be placed on bottom shelves to avoid drips and cross-contamination.

It is recommended that eggs should be refrigerated in order to maintain their freshness and shelf life.

Take care that frozen foods are not stored in the freezer for too long. Blanched vegetables can be stored for one month; beef, lamb, poultry and pork for six months; and unblanched vegetables and fruits in syrup for a year. Oily fish and sausages can be stored for three months. Dairy products can last four to six months, while cakes and pastries can be kept in the freezer for three to six months.

High-risk Foods

Certain foods may carry risks to people who are considered vulnerable, such as the elderly, the ill, pregnant or breastfeeding women, babies, young infants and those suffering from a recurring illness. It is advisable to avoid those foods listed below, which belong to a higher-risk category.

There is a slight chance that some eggs carry the bacteria salmonella. Cook eggs until both the yolk and the white are firm to eliminate this risk.

Pay particular attention to dishes and products incorporating lightly cooked or raw eggs, which should be eliminated from the diet. Sauces including Hollandaise, mayonnaise, mousses, soufflés and meringues all use raw or lightly cooked eggs, as do custard-based dishes, ice creams and sorbets. These are all considered high-risk foods to the vulnerable groups mentioned above.

Certain meats and poultry also carry the potential risk of salmonella and so should be cooked thoroughly until the juices run clear and there is no pinkness left. Unpasteurised products such as milk, cheese (especially soft cheese), pâté and meat (both raw and cooked) all have the potential risk of listeria and should be avoided.

When buying seafood, buy from a reputable source which has a high turnover to ensure freshness. Fish should have bright, clear eyes, shiny skin and bright pink or red gills. The fish should feel stiff to the touch, with a slight smell of sea air and iodine. The flesh of fish steaks and fillets should be translucent, with no signs of discolouration.

Molluscs such as scallops, clams and mussels are sold fresh and are still alive. Avoid any that are open or do not close when tapped lightly. In the same way, univalves such as whelks or winkles should withdraw back into their shells when lightly prodded. When choosing cephalopods such as squid and octopus, they should have a firm flesh and pleasant sea smell.

As with all fish, whether it is shellfish or wet fish, care is required when freezing it. It is imperative to check whether the fish has been frozen before. If it has been frozen, then it should not be frozen again under any circumstances.

Hygiene in the Kitchen

How to Make Pasta

Home-made pasta has a light, almost silky texture and is very different from the fresh pasta that you can buy vacuum packed in supermarkets. It is also surprisingly easy to make and little equipment is needed; just a rolling pin and a sharp knife, although if you make pasta regularly it is worth investing in a pasta machine.

Making Basic Egg Pasta Dough

Ingredients

225 g/8 oz type 001 pasta flour,
plus extra for dusting
1 tsp salt
2 eggs, plus 1 egg yolk
1 tbsp olive oil
1–3 tsp cold water

1   Sift the flour and salt into a mound on a clean work surface and make a well in the middle, keeping the sides quite high, so that the egg mixture will not trickle out when added.

2   Beat together the eggs, yolk, oil and 1 teaspoon of water. Add to the well, then gradually work in the flour, adding extra water if needed, to make a soft but not sticky dough.

3   Knead on a lightly floured surface for 5 minutes, or until the dough is smooth and elastic. Wrap in clingfilm and leave to rest for 20 minutes at room temperature.

Using a Food Processor

Sift the flour and salt into the bowl of a food processor fitted with a metal blade. Add the eggs, yolk, oil and water and pulse-blend until the ingredients are mixed and until the dough begins to come together, adding the extra water if needed. Knead for 1–2 minutes, then wrap and rest as before.

Rolling Pasta by Hand

1   Unwrap the pasta dough and cut in half. Work with just half at a time and keep the other half wrapped in clingfilm.

2   Place the dough on a large, clean work surface lightly dusted with flour, then flatten with your hand and start to roll out. Always roll away from you, starting from the centre and giving the dough a quarter turn after each rolling. Sprinkle a little more flour over the dough if it starts to get sticky.

3   Continue rolling and turning until the dough is as thin as possible; ideally about 3 mm/ 1/8 inch. Make sure that you roll it evenly, or some shapes will cook faster than others.

Rolling Pasta by Machine

A machine makes smoother, thinner, more-even pasta than that made by hand-rolling. Most pasta machines work in the same way but check the manufacturers' instructions.

1   Clamp the machine securely and attach the handle. Set the rollers at their widest setting and sprinkle lightly with flour. Cut the pasta into four pieces. Wrap 3 of them in clingfilm and reserve.

How to Make Pasta

2   Flatten the unwrapped pasta dough slightly, then feed it through the rollers. Fold the strip of dough in 3, rotate and feed through the rollers a second time. Continue to roll the pasta this way, narrowing the roller setting by one notch every second time and flouring the rollers if the pasta starts to get sticky. Only fold the dough the first time it goes through each roller width. The dough will get longer and thinner with every rolling – if it gets too difficult to handle, cut the strip in half and work with 1 piece at a time.

3   If making spaghetti or noodles such as tagliatelle, the second last setting is generally used. For pasta shapes and filled pastas, the dough should be rolled to the finest setting.

4   Fresh pasta should be dried slightly before cutting. Either drape over a narrow wooden pole for 5 minutes or place on a clean tea towel sprinkled with a little flour for 10 minutes.

You can also buy electric pasta machines that carry out the whole pasta-making process, from dough mixing and kneading, to extruding it through cutters into the required shapes – all you have to do is weigh out and add the individual ingredients. They can make over 900 g/2 lb of pasta at a time, but are expensive to buy and take up a lot of space.

Shaping Up

When cutting and shaping freshly made pasta, have 2 or 3 lightly floured tea-towels ready. Arrange the pasta in a single layer, spaced slightly apart, or you may find that they stick together. When they are dry, you can freeze them successfully for up to 6 weeks, by layering in suitable freezer containers between sheets of baking parchment. Spread them out on baking parchment for about 20 minutes, or slightly longer if stuffed, before cooking. When making pasta, do not throw away the trimmings. They can be cut into tiny shapes or thin slivers and used in soups.

∾ **Farfalle** – Use a fluted pasta wheel to cut the pasta sheets into rectangles about 2.5 x 5 cm/ 1 x 12 inches. Pinch the long sides of each rectangle in the middle to make a bow. Spread out on a floured tea towel and leave to dry for at least 15 minutes.

∾ **Lasagne** – This is one of the easiest to make. Simply trim the pasta sheets until neat and cut into lengths the same size as your lasagne dish. Spread the cut sheets on tea towels sprinkled with flour.

∾ **Macaroni** – This is the generic name for hollow pasta. Cut the rolled-out pasta dough into squares, then wrap each around a chopstick, thick skewer or similar, starting from one of the corners. Slip the pasta off, curve slightly if liked and leave to dry for at least 15 minutes.

∾ **Noodles** – If using a pasta machine, use the cutter attachment to produce tagliatelle or fettucine, or use a narrower one for tagliarini or spaghetti. To make by hand, sprinkle the rolled-out pasta with flour, then roll up like a Swiss roll and cut into thin slices. The thickness of these depends on the noodles required. For linguine, cut into 5 mm/¼ inch slices and for tagliatelle cut into 8 mm/⅓ inch slices. Unravel them immediately after cutting. To make thicker ribbon pasta such as pappardelle, use a serrated pastry wheel to cut into wide strips. Leave over a wooden pole for up to 5 minutes to dry out.

∾ **Ravioli** – Cut the rolled-out sheet of dough in half widthways. Cover one half with clingfilm to stop it drying out too quickly. Brush the other sheet of dough with beaten egg. Pipe or spoon small mounds – using about 1 teaspoon of filling in even rows, spacing them at 4 cm/1½ inch intervals. Remove the clingfilm from the reserved pasta sheet and using a rolling pin carefully lift over the dough with the filling. Press down firmly between the pockets of filling to push out any air. Finally, cut into squares with a pastry cutter or sharp knife. Leave on a floured tea towel for 45 minutes before cooking.

You can also use a ravioli tray (raviolatore) to produce perfect even-sized ravioli. A sheet of rolled-out dough is laid over the tray, then pressed into the individual compartments. The filling can then be spooned or piped into the indentations and the second sheet of dough placed on top. To create the individual ravioli squares, a rolling pin is gently rolled over the serrated top. These tins are excellent for making small ravioli containing a little filling.

Three or four simple ingredients combined together make the best fillings. Always season generously with salt and freshly ground black pepper and where the filling is soft, stir in a little beaten egg. Why not try chopped cooked spinach, ricotta and freshly grated nutmeg; finely ground turkey, curd cheese, tarragon and Parmesan cheese; white crabmeat with mascarpone, finely grated lemon rind and dill; or ricotta, roasted garlic and fresh herbs.

- Silhouette Pasta – If rolled out very thinly, fresh herb leaves can be sandwiched between 2 layers of pasta for a stunning silhouette effect. Put the pasta through a machine set on the very last setting, so that it is paper-thin. Cut in half and lightly brush 1 piece with water. Arrange individual fresh herb leaves at regular intervals over the moistened pasta (you will need soft herbs for this – flat-leaf parsley, basil and sage are all ideal). Place the second sheet of dry pasta on top and gently press with a rolling pin to seal them together. Sprinkle the pasta with a little flour, then put it through the machine on the second to finest setting. Use a pastry wheel, dipped in flour, to cut around the herb leaves to make squares, or use a round or oval cutter to stamp out the pasta if preferred. Leave to dry on a floured tea towel for 20 minutes before cooking.

- Tortellini – Use a plain biscuit cutter to stamp out rounds of pasta about 5 cm/2 inches in diameter. Lightly brush each with beaten egg, then spoon or pipe about 1 teaspoon of filling into the middle of each round. Fold in half to make a half-moon shape, gently pressing the edges together to seal. Bend the 2 corners round and press together to seal. Allow to dry on a floured tea towel for 30 minutes before cooking. To make tortelloni, use a slightly larger cutter; about 6.5 cm/2 1/2 inches.

Variations

Flavoured pastas are simple and there are dozens of delicious ways that you can change the flavour and colour of pasta. You will find that you get a more-even colour when using a machine, but the speckled appearance of flavoured hand-rolled pasta can be equally attractive.

- **Chilli** – Add 2 teaspoons of crushed, dried red chillies to the egg mixture before you mix with the flour.

- **Herb** – Stir 3 tablespoons of chopped fresh herbs such as basil, parsley, marjoram or sage or 2 tablespoons of finely chopped, strongly-flavoured herbs like thyme or rosemary into the flour.

- **Olive** – Blend 2 tablespoons of black olive paste with the egg mixture, leaving out the water.

- **Porcini** – Soak 15 g/½ oz dried porcini mushrooms in boiling water for 20 minutes. Drain and squeeze out as much water as possible, then chop very finely. Add to the egg mixture. (Reserve the soaking liquor, strain and use to flavour the pasta sauce.)

- **Saffron** – Sift 1 teaspoon of powdered saffron with the flour.

- **Spinach** – Cook 75 g/3 oz prepared spinach in a covered pan with just the water clinging to the leaves, until wilted. Drain and squeeze dry, then chop finely. Add to the egg mixture.

- **Sun-dried Tomato** – Blend 2 tablespoons of sun-dried tomato paste into the egg mixture, leaving out the water.

- **Wholemeal Pasta** – Substitute half the wholemeal flour for half of the white flour and add an extra 1–2 teaspoons water to the mixture.

How to Make Pasta

Pasta Varieties

asta has been twisted and curled into an unimaginable number of shapes. There is a vast range of both fresh and dried pasta; short and long, tiny varieties for soup, larger ones for stuffing and more unusual designer shapes and flavours.

Dried Pastas

- **Buckwheat Pasta** – Darker in colour than wholewheat pasta, this is made from buckwheat flour. It is gluten-free so is suitable for people who are intolerant to wheat products. Pizzoccheri are thin, flat noodles twisted into nests and are the most common type of buckwheat pasta.

- **Corn Pasta** – Now found on most supermarket shelves, corn pasta is made with maize flour and the plain variety is a bright yellow colour. Like buckwheat pasta, it is gluten-free. When cooking, make sure you use a large saucepan as it tends to cause the water to foam more than ordinary wheat pasta.

- **Coloured and Flavoured Pasta** – The varieties of these types of pasta are endless. The most popular and easily obtainable are spinach and tomato. Often three colours (white, red and green) are packed together and labelled 'tricolore'. Others available in larger food stores and delicatessens include beetroot, saffron, herb, poppy seed, garlic, chilli, mushroom, smoked saffron and black ink. More unusual types such as blue curaco liqueur pasta, which has a bright turquoise colour, have also been created.

- **Durum Wheat Pasta** – This is the most readily available and may be made with or without eggs. Generally plain wheat pasta is used for long, straight shapes such as spaghetti, whereas pasta containing eggs is slightly more fragile, so is packed into nests or waves. Look for the words 'Durum wheat' or 'pasta di semola di grano duro' on the packet when buying, as pastas made from soft wheat tend to become soggy when cooked.

- **Wholewheat Pasta** – Made with wholemeal flour, this has a higher fibre content than ordinary pasta which gives it a slightly chewy texture, nutty flavour and rich brown colour. Wholewheat pasta takes longer to cook, however, than the refined version. We tend to think of it as a modern product associated with the growth in interest of health foods, but it has been made in north-eastern Italy for hundreds of years, where it is known as bigoli and is like a thick spaghetti.

Pasta Shapes

Long Pasta

- **Spaghetti** – Probably the best known type of pasta, spaghetti derives its name from the word *spago* meaning string, which describes its round, thin shape perfectly. Spaghettini is a thinner variety and spaghettoni is thicker. Vermicelli is a very fine type of spaghetti.

- **Tagliatelle** – Tagliatelle is the most common type of ribbon-noodle pasta and each ribbon of pasta is usually slightly less than 1 cm/1/2 inch wide. It is traditionally from Bologna where it always accompanies bolognaise sauce (rather than spaghetti). It is sold coiled into nests that unravel when cooked. Thinner varieties of tagliarini or tagliolini are also available. A mixture of

Pasta Varieties

white and spinach-flavoured tagliatelle is known as *paglia e fieno* which translates as straw and hay. Fettucine is the Roman version of tagliatelle and is cut slightly thinner.

∾ Ziti – Long, thick and hollow, ziti may be ridged but is usually smooth. It takes its name from zita, meaning fiancee, as it was once traditional to serve it at weddings in southern Italy. Zitoni is a similar larger pasta; mezza zita is thinner.

Short Pasta

There are basically two types of short pasta: secca is factory-made from durum wheat and water, which is pressed into assorted shapes and sizes, and pasta all'uovo is made with eggs, which is particularly popular in northern Italy, where it is served with meat or creamy sauces. Pasta all'uovo is slightly more expensive than plain pasta, but cooks in less time and is less likely to go soggy if overcooked. It is also much more nutritious and has an attractive golden colour. There are hundreds of different shapes and some of the most popular ones are listed below.

∾ Conchiglie – As the name implies, these pasta shapes resemble conch shells and are ideal for serving with thinner sauces which will get trapped in the shells. Sizes vary from very tiny ones to large ones which are suitable for stuffing. They may be smooth or ridged conchiglie rigate.

∾ Eliche and Fusilli – These are twisted into the shape of a screw, which is where their name comes from. Eliche is often wrongly labelled as fusilli as the two are similar, but fusilli is more tightly coiled and opens out slightly during cooking.

∾ Farfalle – A popular pasta shape, these are bow or butterfly shaped, often with crinkled edges.

∾ Gnocchi Sardi – These come from Sardinia and are named after the little gnocchi potato dumplings. Often served with rich meat sauces, they have a somewhat chewy texture.

- Macaroni – This is known as *maccheroni* in Italy. You may find it labelled as 'elbow macaroni' which describes its shape (although it is sometimes almost straight). This was once the most popular imported pasta and is particularly good in baked dishes, notably macaroni cheese. A thin, quick-cook variety is also available.

- Penne Slightly larger, hollow tubes than macaroni, the ends are cut diagonally and are pointed like quills. There are also less well-known varieties including the thinner pennette and even thinner pennini. They are often made with egg or flavoured with tomato or spinach.

- Pipe This is curved, hollow pasta and is often sold ridged as 'pipe rigate'. The smaller type is known as 'pipette'.

- Rigatoni This is substantial, chunky, tubular pasta and is often used for baking. Because the pasta is thick, it tends to be slightly chewier than other short pastas. Rigatoni goes well with meat and strongly flavoured sauces.

- Rotelle This is thin, wheel-shaped pasta, also known as 'ruote' and often sold in packets of two or three colours.

Flat Pasta

There are many types of long, flat ribbon pastas, but there is only one flat pasta – lasagne – which is usually used for baking in the oven (al forno). These thin sheets are layered up with a sauce or may be curled into large tubes about 10 cm/4 inches long to make cannelloni. In Italy, cannelloni are usually made from fresh sheets of lasagne rolled around the filling, however, dried tubes are easily available and simple to use. Three flavours of lasagne are available: plain, spinach or wholewheat. Most sheets are flat, but some have curled edges which help trap the sauce during cooking and stop it running to the bottom of the dish. Lasagnette are long, narrow

Pasta Varieties

strips of flat pasta and are crimped on one or both long edges. Like lasagne, they are designed to be layered up with a sauce and baked.

Stuffed Pasta

Tortellini are the most common of dried pasta shapes and consist of tiny, stuffed pieces of pasta which are folded, and then the ends are joined to make a ring. A speciality of Bologna, larger ones are made from rounds or squares and are joined without leaving a hole in the middle. They are called tortelloni and generally are made with a meat (*alla carne*) or cheese (*ai formaggi*) filling and will keep for up to a year (but always check the sell-by date). Cappelletti, ravioli and agnalotti are sometimes sold dried, but more often fresh.

Soup Pasta

Tiny pasta shapes known as *pastina* in Italy come in hundreds of different shapes and are often added to soups. Risi is the smallest type of pasta and looks like grains of rice, whereas orzi, another soup pasta, resembles barley. Slightly larger ones include, stellette (stars), and rotelli (wheels). Many are miniature shapes of larger pasta, such as farfallette (little bows) and conchigliette (little shells).

Fresh Pasta

Fresh pasta has become increasingly popular over the past decade and can be found in the chilled cabinets of supermarkets, as well as being sold loose in specialist shops. Ideally, you should buy fresh pasta on the day you are going to cook it, or use within a day or two. It must be stored in the refrigerator until you are ready to use it, as it contains eggs, which shorten its keeping time. It is generally available in the same shapes as dried pasta, but has a much greater range of stuffed fillings. Ravioli is one of the most common. It is shaped into large squares with fluted edges and is made with many different pasta doughs including saffron and fresh herbs. The fillings may be anything, for example, spinach and ricotta, mushroom, fish and shellfish, meat, but especially chicken. They may also be shaped into long rectangles, circles or ovals.

Oriental Noodles

Pasta originated in China and not in Italy, so it is hardly surprising that there is a vast range of oriental noodles.

- ∞ **Buckwheat Noodles** Soba are the most common and are a dark, greyish-brown colour. They feature in Japanese cooking in soups and stir-fries.

- ∞ **Cellophane Noodles** Made from mung beans, these are translucent, flavourless noodles and are only available dried. They are never boiled and simply need soaking in very hot water.

- ∞ **Egg Noodles** Commonly used in Chinese cooking, they come in several thicknesses; thin and medium being the most popular.

- ∞ **Rice Noodles** These are fine, delicate, opaque noodles which are made from rice and are a popular ingredient in Thai and Malaysian cooking.

- ∞ **Udon Noodles** These are thick Japanese noodles which can be round or flat and are available both fresh, dried or precooked.

Pasta Varieties

Pasta Techniques Tips

C

Steps to Cooking Perfect Pasta

Follow a few simple rules to ensure that your pasta is cooked to perfection every time:

1   Choose a big saucepan – there needs to be plenty of room for the pasta to move around during cooking so that it does not stick together. The most convenient type of saucepan has a built-in perforated inner pan, so that the pasta can be lifted out of the water and drained as soon as it is cooked.

2   Cook the pasta in a large quantity of fast-boiling, well-salted water; ideally about 4 litres/7 pints of water and 1^1/$_2$ –2 tablespoons of salt for every 350 g/12 oz–450 g/1 lb of pasta. Some cooks say that the addition of 1–2 teaspoons of olive or sunflower oil not only helps to stop the water boiling over but also helps to prevent the pasta from sticking. However, other cooks believe that as long as the saucepan is large enough and the water is on a full-rolling boil, the pasta will not stick together nor will the water boil over.

3   Tip in the pasta all at once, give it a stir and cover with a lid. Quickly bring back to a rolling boil then remove the lid – do not cover with a lid during cooking. Once it is boiling, turn down the heat to medium-high and cook the pasta for the required time. It should be *al dente* which literally translates as 'to the tooth' and means that the pasta should be tender, but still firm to the bite. Test frequently towards the end of cooking time; the only way to do this is to take out a piece and try it. Stir the pasta occasionally during cooking with a wooden spoon or fork to make sure that it does not stick to the pan.

4   As soon as the pasta is ready, drain in a colander (or by lifting the draining pan up and out of the water if you have a pasta pot with an inner drainer). Give it a shake, so that any trapped water can drain out. At this stage you can toss the pasta in a little oil or butter if you are not mixing it with a sauce. Reserve a little of the cooking water to stir into the pasta, this not only helps to thin the sauce if necessary, but also helps prevent the cooked pasta sticking together as it cools.

Some pastas need a little more care when cooking than others. Never stir stuffed pastas vigorously, or they may split open and the filling will be lost in the cooking water. When cooking long, dried pasta such as spaghetti, you will need to coil the pasta into the water as it starts to soften. Hold one end of the strands of spaghetti and push the other to the bottom of the pan, coiling them round, and using a wooden spoon or fork, when the boiling water gets too close to your hand.

An alternative cooking method is to add the pasta to boiling salted water as before, then boil rapidly for 2 minutes. Cover the pan with a tight-fitting lid and turn off the heat. Leave to stand for the full cooking time, then drain and serve in the usual way. Pasta may also be cooked successfully in a microwave, although it does not cook any faster than on the hob. Put the pasta in a large bowl, add salt, then pour over enough boiling water to cover the pasta by at least 2.5 cm/1 inch. Microwave on High (100% power) for the times given below. Allow the pasta to stand for 2–3 minutes before draining.

Pasta Cooking Times

Start timing from the moment that the pasta returns to the boil; not from when it was added. Use a kitchen timer if possible, as even a few seconds too long may spoil the pasta.

Pasta Techniques & Tips

Fresh 2–3 minutes for thin noodles (although very fine pastas may be ready within seconds of the pasta boiling), 3–4 minutes for thick noodles and shapes and 5–7 minutes for filled pastas.

Dried 8–12 minutes; filled pastas can take up to 20 minutes to cook, however, you should always check the packet instructions, as some pastas labelled 'quick cook' only take about 4 minutes.

Serving Quantities

As an approximate guide, allow 75–125 g (3–4 oz) uncooked pasta per person. Obviously the amount will depend on whether the pasta is being served for a light or main meal and the type of sauce that it is being served with.

Matching Pasta Types and Sauces

It is entirely up to you which pasta you serve with which sauce but, in general, heavier sauces with large chunks of meat or vegetables go less with pastas that will trap the sauce and meat in curls and hollows, such as penne, shells, riagatoni or spirals. On the other hand, soft fluid sauces suit long pastas such as linguine, pappardelle, or tagliatelle.

Classic Sauces

- Alla Carbonara Pasta with ham, eggs and cream – the heat of the pasta cooks the eggs to thicken the sauce.

- Alla Napoletana Made from fresh tomatoes, but with olive oil, garlic and onions.

- ❧ **All'arrabiata** A hot sauce with red chillies, tomatoes and chopped bacon.

- ❧ **All'aglio e Olio** Pasta with olive oil and finely chopped garlic.

- ❧ **Alla Marinara** A fresh tomato and basil sauce, sometimes with wine (not seafood).

- ❧ **Con Ragù** Meat sauce from Bologna (known as bolognaise sauce in English), often made with half minced pork and half minced beef. This is traditionally served with tagliatelle and not spaghetti.

Serving Pasta

In Italy, pasta is usually dressed with the sauce before serving to combine the flavours, but you can top the pasta with the sauce if you prefer, in which case, toss it in a little olive oil or butter to give it an attractive sheen. Cook the sauce and pasta so that they will both be ready at the same time; most sauces can be left to stand for a few minutes and reheated when the pasta is ready. If the pasta is ready before the sauce, drain it, and return to the pan with a tight-fitting lid – it should be fine for a few minutes. Always serve in warmed serving bowls or plates, as pasta loses heat very quickly.

Serving Wines with Pasta

If possible, choose a wine that comes from the same region as the dish you are serving. If there is wine in the sauce, you will be able to serve the rest of the bottle with your meal, so make sure you choose one that you enjoy drinking. Otherwise, pick a wine that matches the strongest-flavoured ingredient in the sauce. Rich, meaty sauces or highly spiced ones with lots of garlic need a robust, full-bodied wine to go with them. Of course, there is no reason why you should stick to Italian wines and if you are serving an oriental pasta dish you may opt for lager or other drinks. Below are ten well-known types of Italian wine.

Pasta Techniques & Tips

White Wines

- **Chardonnay** This wine is produced in many parts of the world and is wonderful served with fish dishes. The Italian chardonnay has a faint lemony flavour.

- **Frascati** This wine is made near Rome and is one of the most popular Italian wines. It is crisp and fruity and has quite a lot of body. It goes well with most foods.

- **Orvieto** This wine is named after the town of the same name, just north of Rome. It is dry and soft with a slightly nutty and fruity flavour and is good for summer drinking and serving with fish and white meats.

- **Soave** This wine is one of Italy's most famous wines. The best ones have a distinct hint of almonds and are dry and crisp. It goes well with shellfish, chicken and light vegetable pasta sauces.

- **Verdicchio** This wine comes in a carved amphora bottle and in Italy is known as La Lollobrigida. A crisp, clean and dry white wine with a slightly metallic edge, it is best when served with fish and seafood.

Red Wines

- **Barbaresco** This wine is full-bodied with an intense flavour and a high tannin content. It teams well with rich pasta dishes, especially beef.

- **Bardolino** This is light and fruity with an almost cherry and slightly bitter almond taste; perfect for duck and game.

- **Barolo** This is one of Italy's finest wines and is a full-bodied red. Serve with rich meaty dishes, game or spicy sausage pasta sauces.

~ Chianti This wine is best drunk when young and may be served slightly chilled. It is often regarded as the classic accompaniment to pasta.

Pasta Equipment

When making and cooking pasta, a bare minimum of equipment is needed; some would say that a rolling pin, a large pan and a colander would suffice, however, there are many gadgets that make the process a lot easier.

When Making

~ Rolling Pin Try to use one that is quite slender and choose a conventional wooden one without handles. In Italy pasta rolling pins are very long, for rolling out large quantities of pasta at a time, and slightly thicker in the middle with tapering ends.

~ Pasta Machine A traditional, hand-cranked pasta machine has adjusting rollers and usually cutters for making tagliatelle and finer tagliarini. More complicated ones come with a selection of cutters.

~ Pasta Wheel This is useful for cutting noodles such as tagliatelle and pappardelle if you do not have a pasta machine and also for stuffed shapes such as ravioli. This is an inexpensive piece of equipment and less likely to drag or tear the pasta than a knife.

Pasta Techniques & Tips

❧ Ravioli Cutter Specially designed, fluted-edged cutters can be bought for cutting pasta. A fluted or plain biscuit cutter works just as well.

When Cooking and Serving

❧ Long-handled Pasta Fork This is useful for stirring the pasta to keep the pieces separate during cooking. You can also get wooden pasta hooks which will lift out the strands of pasta so that you can check whether or not it is cooked.

❧ Parmesan Graters These range from simple hand graters to electrical gadgets. If sharp, the fine side of a box grater works equally well.

❧ Parmesan Knife This is used to shave Parmesan off a block. A vegetable peeler may be used as an alternative.

❧ Pasta Cooking Pot Officially this should be tall with straight sides and handles and should have an inner basket. When buying, choose one that is not too heavy, and will be easy to manage when full.

❧ Pasta measure This is a wooden, plastic or metal gadget with several holes for measuring spaghetti. Each hole takes a different amount of pasta for a given number of people. It's a great way to control potion sizes that can all too easily become too large.

Pasta Pantry

Ingredients for Making Egg Pasta

Only four simple ingredients are needed for basic pasta dough: flour, eggs, olive oil and salt.

- **Eggs** These should be as fresh as possible and preferably free-range which tend to have deeper-coloured yolks, and therefore, give the pasta a richer, more golden colour. They should be kept at room temperature and not used straight from the refrigerator when making pasta.

- **Flour** The best flour for pasta is Farina Bianca 00 or Tipo 00 and can be bought from Italian food stores. This type of flour is a very fine wheat flour imported from Italy. You can use strong, white bread flour as an alternative, but the dough will be more difficult to roll out, especially if you are making the pasta by hand.

- **Olive Oil** Strictly speaking, this is not essential for pasta but it gives the dough flavour and makes it slightly softer and therefore easier to roll. Olive oil varies in flavour and colour, depending on where it comes from. Generally, those from hotter climates such as southern Italy and Spain have a stronger flavour and darker colour than those from areas such as as France. Pure or light olive oil is refined to remove any impurities, is then blended and has a light flavour. Virgin olive oil is a pure first-pressed oil, and extra-virgin is a superior product which comes from the first cold pressing of the olives and must have a low acidity; less than 1 per cent.

- **Salt** Vital for flavour and should be finely ground, whether ordinary or sea salt.

Ingredients for Pasta Sauces

∞ **Anchovies** These are small, silvery fish that grow up to 10 cm/4 inches long and for centuries have been preserved in salt. They are generally bought as fillets in small cans of around 50 g/ 2 oz. When chopped and mixed with olive oil and garlic, they make an excellent, simple pasta sauce. They are very salty, so bear this in mind when adding seasoning, or if other salty ingredients are being used. Anchovies should be soaked in a little milk or water for about 20 minutes before using.

∞ **Capers** These are the green flower buds of a bush that grows around the shores of the Mediterranean and they add a sharp piquancy to sauces. Most are sold bottled in vinegar which makes them particularly good with fish and seafood. If you buy salted capers, rinse them thoroughly, then soak for a few minutes to remove excess salt.

∞ **Cheeses** Many cheeses feature in pasta dishes, but you do not have to stick to Italian varieties. However, these naturally go well with Italian-flavoured pasta dishes. Gorgonzola is a blue-veined cheese from Lombardy. It melts quickly, so is good in sauces and is also used for stuffing pastas such as ravioli. Mascarpone is a rich, fresh creamy cheese that melts without curdling. It can be added to pasta with fresh herbs to make a quick sauce. Parmesan is often grated over pasta dishes or shaved into paper-thin curls when serving. Ricotta is a fresh, soft white cheese that melts beautifully. It has a somewhat bland taste, so is most often combined with other ingredients, such as fresh herbs.

❧ Herbs Both fresh and dried herbs enhance pasta dishes. Those most frequently used are basil, bay leaves, coriander, dill, oregano and marjoram, parsley, rosemary and thyme. Basil has a natural affinity with tomatoes and its sweet, fragrant flavour counteracts any acidity. Although basil originated in India, the Italians grow it prolifically. It should be torn or shredded and added at the last moment so that it retains its bright green colour and pungent flavour. Dried basil is a poor substitute for fresh – it is better to add a spoonful of green pesto. Look out for a recent addition, purple-coloured basil, which looks especially attractive when used as a garnish on simple dishes such as pasta tossed in olive oil, garlic and cheese.

Bay leaves are often used to flavour white sauces and meat dishes such as bolognaise. They are always removed before serving, although fresh ones make an attractive garnish. Coriander is rarely used in Italian pasta dishes, but is often used in oriental noodle dishes. Dill, with its feathery leaves and aniseed flavour, is used a lot in fish and seafood dishes. Oregano and marjoram are frequently used with tomatoes. Oregano is the wild strain and has a less delicate flavour than marjoram, although the two are interchangeable in dishes.

Recently, curly-leafed parsley has been upstaged by flat-leaf, also known as Italian or Continental parsley, although either can be used. Rosemary is probably the most pungent herb available and should be used sparingly. Either remove the leaves from the sprig or add the whole sprig to sauces, then remove at the end of cooking and discard.

Thyme is a strongly flavoured herb and although it is better fresh, dried makes a reasonable substitute. It goes well in meat and strongly flavoured dishes. Always strip the leaves off the woody stem before chopping.

❧ Mushrooms There are many varieties of fresh, cultivated and wild mushrooms that feature in pasta sauces. Dried porcini mushrooms are also often used for their intense flavour. Only a very small amount is needed; 10-15 g/½ oz is enough for a dish to serve four people. Always soak them first in warm water, then strain the soaking liquid to remove any grit and add to the sauce as well as the mushrooms.

❧ Olives Both black and green olives are used in sauces. Sometimes they are chopped, but more often are used whole (but make sure you stone them first). Buy plain ones in olive oil for adding to sauces; the small shiny ones have the best flavour and should be added at the end of cooking time, or they may become slightly bitter.

❧ Pesto The best pesto is most definetly homemade – there is no substitute. Blend fresh basil leaves with olive oil, pine nuts and freshly grated Parmesan cheese. Some supermarkets, however, sell fresh pesto in tubs in the chilled cabinet. The bottled varieties come as green and red (which is made from sun-dried tomatoes and red peppers). Pesto adds richness and flavour to sauces, or may be used on its own, simply tossed with cooked pasta.

❧ Pine Nuts A vital ingredient of pesto, these small, creamy white nuts have a buttery texture and a hint of pine resin. Buy in small quantities and store in the refrigerator.

❧ Spices Often added to pasta dishes, most notably to those made with Eastern noodles. They include chillies, garlic and saffron. Small red chillies are popular in pasta dishes from southern Italy, but are usually added in small quantities to enhance flavour, rather than to make them hot and fiery. Garlic should be used in small quantities to enhance flavour. The combination of olive oil and garlic forms the basis of many pasta sauces. The longer garlic is cooked the more mellow the flavour. When buying, look for heads which are firm and showing no signs of sprouting; larger cloves have a sweeter flavour. Saffron is the world's most expensive spice. The stigmas are gathered from the saffron crocus and just a pinch will add a rich, golden colour and fragrant flavour to your dish – a little saffron goes a long way.

∾ Tomatoes Many tomato products come from southern Italy where they are ripened on the vine in the hot sun. It is hardly surprising that they feature in so many pasta dishes. The simplest of sauces can be made from canned, peeled plum tomatoes which come whole or chopped and can now be bought with added flavourings such as chilli, basil and peppers. These are excellent when fresh tomatoes are not at their best flavour-wise.

∾ Passata is pulped tomatoes that have been strained to remove the seeds. It comes in cartons and is a useful addition to the storecupboard. Sun-dried tomatoes may be plain, dried or in oil. The dried variety needs re-hydrating. This can be done by chopping the sun-dried tomatoes and adding them to a sauce that needs to be cooked for a long time. If you are making a quick sauce, then soften the sun-dried tomatoes by soaking them in hot water for a couple of hours before using. Sun-dried tomatoes in oil already have a soft texture and are excellent for adding a deep, almost roasted flavour to pasta dishes.

∾ Tomato Purée This is a strong, thick paste made from tomatoes, salt and citric acid. It is sold in tubes and jars – only a little is needed to give your dish a rich, tomato taste. Too much tomato purée can overpower a dish and make it acidic. Sun-dried tomato purée has a sweeter and milder flavour and is a thick mixture of sun-dried tomatoes and olive oil.

∾ Vinegar A dash of red or white wine vinegar may be added to a pasta dish, but the most frequently used in modern cooking is balsamic vinegar (a rich, sweetish, smooth brown vinegar aged in wooden barrels until the flavour is very mellow). The best balsamic vinegars are matured for 40 years upwards and are therefore very expensive. Cheaper ones sold in supermarkets have been aged for four to five years and are perfect for adding to sauces.

Pasta Pantry

Starters

Far from being only a main meal staple, pasta also makes a great basis for many exciting and inventive starter dishes – which is how the Italians eat it after all! Whether a small portion of a pasta medley such as Louisiana Prawns & Fettucine or a warming soup such as Pasta & Bean Soup, the recipes in this chapter are sure to start off any meal with a tasty bang!

Fresh Tagliatelle with Courgettes

Serves 4–6

225 g /8 oz strong plain bread flour
or type 00 pasta flour, plus extra
for rolling
1 tsp salt
2 medium eggs
1 medium egg yolk
3 tbsp extra virgin olive oil
2 small courgettes, halved
lengthwise and thinly sliced
2 garlic cloves, peeled and
thinly sliced
large pinch chilli flakes
zest of $\frac{1}{2}$ lemon
1 tbsp freshly shredded basil
salt and freshly ground
black pepper
freshly grated Parmesan cheese,
to serve

Sift the flour and salt into a large bowl, make a well in the centre and add the eggs and yolk, 1 tablespoon of oil with 1 teaspoon of water. Gradually mix to form a soft but not sticky dough, adding a little more flour or water as necessary. Turn out on to a lightly floured surface and knead for 5 minutes, or until smooth and elastic. Wrap in clingfilm and leave to rest at room temperature for about 30 minutes. Divide the dough into eight pieces. Feed a piece through the pasta machine. Gradually decrease the settings on the rollers, feeding the pasta through each time, until the sheet is very long and thin. If the pasta seems sticky, dust the work surface and both sides of the pasta generously with flour. Cut in half crosswise and hang over a clean pole. Repeat with the remaining dough. Leave to dry for about 5 minutes. Feed each sheet through the tagliatelle cutter, hanging the cut pasta over the pole. Leave to dry for a further 5 minutes. Wind a handful of pasta strands into nests and leave on a floured tea towel. Repeat with the remaining dough and leave to dry for 5 minutes.

Cook the pasta in plenty of salted boiling water for 2–3 minutes, or until *al dente*. Meanwhile, heat the remaining oil in a large frying pan and add the courgettes, garlic, chilli and lemon zest. Cook over a medium heat for 3–4 minutes, or until the courgettes are lightly golden and tender. Drain the pasta thoroughly, reserving 2 tablespoons of the cooking water. Add the pasta to the courgettes with the basil and seasoning. Mix well, adding the reserved cooking water. Serve with the Parmesan cheese.

Beetroot Ravioli
with Dill Cream Sauce

Serves 4–6

fresh pasta (*see* Fresh Tagliatelle
with Courgettes, page 40)
1 tbsp olive oil
1 small onion, peeled and
finely chopped
$\frac{1}{2}$ tsp caraway seeds
175 g/6 oz cooked beetroot,
chopped
175 g/6 oz ricotta cheese
25 g/1 oz fresh white breadcrumbs
1 medium egg yolk
2 tbsp grated Parmesan cheese
salt and freshly ground
black pepper
4 tbsp walnut oil
4 tbsp freshly chopped dill
1 tbsp green peppercorns,
drained and roughly chopped
6 tbsp crème fraîche

Make the pasta dough according to the recipe on page 40. Wrap in clingfilm and leave to rest for 30 minutes.

Heat the olive oil in a large frying pan, add the onion and caraway seeds and cook over a medium heat for 5 minutes, or until the onion is softened and lightly golden. Stir in the beetroot and cook for 5 minutes. Blend the beetroot mixture in a food processor until smooth, then allow to cool. Stir in the ricotta cheese, breadcrumbs, egg yolk and Parmesan cheese. Season to taste with salt and pepper, and reserve.

Divide the pasta dough into 8 pieces. Roll out as for tagliatelle, but do not cut the sheets in half. Lay 1 sheet on a floured surface and place 5 heaped teaspoons of the filling 2.5 cm/1 inch apart. Dampen around the heaps of filling and lay a second sheet of pasta over the top. Press around the heaps to seal. Cut into squares using a pastry wheel or sharp knife. Put the filled pasta shapes on to a floured tea towel.

Bring a large pan of lightly salted water to a rolling boil. Drop the ravioli into the boiling water, return to the boil and cook for 3–4 minutes, until *al dente*. Meanwhile, heat the walnut oil in a small pan then add the dill and green peppercorns. Remove from the heat, stir in the crème fraîche and season well. Drain the cooked pasta thoroughly and toss with the sauce. Tip into warmed serving dishes and serve immediately.

Gnocchi with Grilled Cherry Tomato Sauce

Serves 4

450 g/1 lb floury potatoes, unpeeled
1 medium egg
1 tsp salt
75–90 g/3–3 $^1/_2$ oz plain flour
450 g/1 lb mixed red and orange cherry tomatoes, halved lengthways
2 garlic cloves, peeled and finely sliced
zest of $^1/_2$ lemon, finely grated
1 tbsp freshly chopped thyme
1 tbsp freshly chopped basil
2 tbsp extra virgin olive oil, plus extra for drizzling
salt and freshly ground black pepper
pinch of sugar
freshly grated Parmesan cheese, to serve

Preheat the grill just before required. Bring a large pan of salted water to the boil, add the potatoes and cook for 20–25 minutes until tender. Drain. Leave until cool enough to handle but still hot, then peel them and place in a large bowl. Mash until smooth then work in the egg, salt and enough of the flour to form a soft dough.

With floured hands, roll a spoonful of the dough into a small ball. Flatten the ball slightly on to the back of a large fork, then roll it off the fork to make a little ridged dumpling. Place each gnocchi on to a floured tea towel as you work.

Place the tomatoes in a flameproof shallow dish. Add the garlic, lemon zest, herbs and olive oil. Season to taste with salt and pepper and sprinkle over the sugar. Cook under the preheated grill for 10 minutes, or until the tomatoes are charred and tender, stirring once or twice.

Meanwhile, bring a large pan of lightly salted water to the boil then reduce to a steady simmer. Dropping in 6–8 gnocchi at a time, cook in batches for 3–4 minutes, or until they begin bobbing up to the surface. Remove with a slotted spoon and drain well on absorbent kitchen paper before transferring to a warmed serving dish; cover with foil. Toss the cooked gnocchi with the tomato sauce. Serve immediately with a little grated Parmesan cheese.

Spinach ❧ Ricotta Gnocchi with Butter ❧ Parmesan

Serves 2–4

125 g/4 oz frozen leaf
spinach, thawed
225 g/8 oz ricotta cheese
2 small eggs, lightly beaten
50 g/2 oz freshly grated
Parmesan cheese
salt and freshly ground
black pepper
2 tbsp freshly chopped basil
50 g/2 oz plain flour
50 g/2 oz unsalted butter
2 garlic cloves, peeled and crushed
Parmesan cheese shavings,
to serve

Squeeze the excess moisture from the spinach and chop finely. Blend in a food processor with the ricotta cheese, eggs, Parmesan cheese, seasoning and 1 tablespoon of the basil until smooth. Scrape into a bowl then add sufficient flour to form a soft, slightly sticky dough.

Bring a large pan of salted water to a rolling boil. Transfer the spinach mixture to a piping bag fitted with a large plain nozzle. As soon as the water is boiling, pipe 10–12 short lengths of the mixture into the water, using a sharp knife to cut the gnocchi as you go.

Bring the water back to the boil and cook the gnocchi for 3–4 minutes, or until they begin to rise to the surface. Remove with a slotted spoon, drain on absorbent kitchen paper and transfer to a warmed serving dish. Cook the gnocchi in batches if necessary.

Melt the butter in a small frying pan and when foaming add the garlic and remaining basil. Remove from the heat and immediately pour over the cooked gnocchi. Season well with salt and pepper and serve immediately with extra grated Parmesan cheese.

Tagliatelle with Brown Butter, Asparagus & Parmesan

Serves 6

fresh pasta (*see* Fresh Tagliatelle
with Courgettes, page 40) or
450 g/1 lb dried tagliatelle, such
as the white and green variety
350 g/12 oz asparagus, trimmed
and cut into short lengths
75 g/3 oz unsalted butter
1 garlic clove, peeled and sliced
25 g/1 oz flaked hazelnuts or whole
hazelnuts, roughly chopped
1 tbsp freshly chopped parsley
1 tbsp freshly snipped chives
salt and freshly ground
black pepper
50 g/2 oz freshly grated Parmesan
cheese, to serve

If using fresh pasta, prepare the dough according to the recipe on page 40. Cut into tagliatelle, wind into nests and reserve on a floured tea towel until ready to cook.

Bring a pan of lightly salted water to the boil. Add the asparagus and cook for 1 minute. Drain immediately, refresh under cold running water and drain again. Pat dry and reserve.

Melt the butter in a large frying pan, then add the garlic and hazelnuts and cook over a medium heat until the butter turns golden. Immediately remove from the heat and add the parsley, chives and asparagus. Leave for 2–3 minutes, until the asparagus is heated through.

Meanwhile, bring a large pan of lightly salted water to a rolling boil, then add the pasta nests. Cook until *al dente*: 2–3 minutes for fresh pasta and according to the packet instructions for dried pasta. Drain the pasta thoroughly and return to the pan. Add the asparagus mixture and toss together. Season to taste with salt and pepper and tip into a warmed serving dish. Serve immediately with grated Parmesan cheese.

Pasta with Raw Fennel, Tomato & Red Onions

Serves 6

1 fennel bulb
700 g/1$^{1}/_{2}$ lb tomatoes
1 garlic clove
$^{1}/_{4}$ small red onion
small handful fresh basil
small handful fresh mint
100 ml/3$^{1}/_{2}$ fl oz extra virgin olive
oil, plus extra to serve
juice of 1 lemon
salt and freshly ground
black pepper
450 g/1 lb penne or pennette
freshly grated Parmesan cheese,
to serve

Trim the fennel and slice thinly. Stack the slices and cut into sticks, then cut crosswise again into fine dice. Deseed the tomatoes and chop them finely. Peel and finely chop or crush the garlic. Peel and finely chop or grate the onion.

Stack the basil leaves then roll up tightly. Slice crosswise into fine shreds. Finely chop the mint.

Place the chopped vegetables and herbs in a medium bowl. Add the olive oil and lemon juice and mix together. Season well with salt and pepper then leave for 30 minutes to allow the flavours to develop.

Bring a large pan of salted water to a rolling boil. Add the pasta and cook according to the packet instructions, or until *al dente*.

Drain the cooked pasta thoroughly. Transfer to a warmed serving dish, pour over the vegetable mixture and toss. Serve with the grated Parmesan cheese and extra olive oil to drizzle over.

Spaghetti with Fresh Tomatoes, Chilli ❦ Potatoes

Serves 6

2 medium potatoes, unpeeled
3 garlic cloves, peeled and crushed
1 small bunch basil,
roughly chopped
6 tbsp olive oil
4 large ripe plum tomatoes, skinned,
seeded and chopped
1 small red chilli, deseeded and
finely chopped
salt and freshly ground black pepper
450 g/1 lb spaghetti
4 tbsp freshly grated Parmesan
cheese, to serve (optional)

Preheat the grill to high 5 minutes before using. Cook the potatoes in plenty of boiling water until tender but firm. Allow to cool, then peel and cut into cubes.

Blend the garlic, basil and 4 tablespoons of the olive oil in a blender or food processor until the basil is finely chopped, then reserve.

Place the tomatoes, basil and oil mixture in a small bowl, add the chilli and season with salt and pepper to taste. Mix together and reserve the sauce.

Bring a large pan of salted water to a rolling boil, add the spaghetti and cook according to the packet instructions, or until *al dente*.

Meanwhile, toss the potato cubes with the remaining olive oil and transfer to a baking sheet. Place the potatoes under the preheated grill until they are crisp and golden, turning once or twice, then drain on absorbent kitchen paper.

Drain the pasta thoroughly and transfer to a warmed shallow serving bowl. Add the tomato sauce and the hot potatoes. Toss well and adjust the seasoning to taste. Serve immediately with the grated Parmesan cheese, if using.

Pasta Genovese with Pesto, Green Beans ❧ Potatoes

Serves 6

40 g/1½ oz basil leaves
2 garlic cloves, peeled
and crushed
2 tbsp pine nuts, lightly toasted
25 g/1 oz freshly grated
Parmesan cheese
75 ml/3 fl oz extra virgin olive oil
salt and freshly ground pepper
175 g/6 oz new potatoes,
scrubbed
125 g/4 oz fine French
beans, trimmed
2 tbsp olive oil
450 g/1 lb pasta shapes
extra freshly grated Parmesan
cheese, to serve

Put the basil leaves, garlic, pine nuts and Parmesan cheese into a food processor and blend until finely chopped. Transfer the mixture in to a small bowl and stir in the olive oil. Season the pesto to taste with salt and pepper and reserve.

Bring a pan of salted water to a rolling boil and cook the potatoes for 12–14 minutes, or until tender. About 4 minutes before the end of the cooking time, add the beans. Drain well and refresh under cold water. Reserve the beans and slice the potatoes thickly, or halve them if small.

Heat the olive oil in a frying pan and add the potatoes. Fry over a medium heat for 5 minutes, or until golden. Add the reserved beans and pesto and cook for a further 2 minutes.

Meanwhile, bring a large pan of lightly salted water to a rolling boil. Cook the pasta shapes according to the packet instructions, or until *al dente*. Drain thoroughly, return to the pan and add the pesto mixture. Toss well and heat through for 1–2 minutes. Tip into a warmed serving bowl and serve immediately with Parmesan cheese.

Tiny Pasta with Fresh Herb Sauce

Serves 6

375 g/13 oz tripolini (small bows with
rounded ends) or small farfalle
2 tbsp freshly chopped flat
leaf parsley
2 tbsp freshly chopped basil
1 tbsp freshly snipped chives
1 tbsp freshly chopped chervil
1 tbsp freshly chopped tarragon
1 tbsp freshly chopped sage
1 tbsp freshly chopped oregano
1 tbsp freshly chopped marjoram
1 tbsp freshly chopped thyme
1 tbsp freshly chopped rosemary
finely grated zest of 1 lemon
75 ml/3 fl oz extra virgin olive oil
2 garlic cloves, peeled and
finely chopped
1/2 tsp dried chilli flakes
salt and freshly ground
black pepper
freshly grated Parmesan cheese,
to serve

Bring a large pan of lightly salted water to a rolling boil. Add the pasta and cook according to the packet instructions, or until *al dente*.

Meanwhile, place all the herbs, the lemon zest, olive oil, garlic and chilli flakes in a heavy-based pan. Heat gently for 2–3 minutes, or until the herbs turn bright green and become very fragrant. Remove from the heat and season to taste with salt and pepper.

Drain the pasta thoroughly, reserving 2–3 tablespoons of the cooking water. Transfer the pasta to a large warmed bowl.

Pour the heated herb mixture over the pasta and toss together until thoroughly mixed. Check and adjust the seasoning, adding a little of the pasta cooking water if the pasta mixture seems a bit dry. Transfer to warmed serving dishes and serve immediately with freshly grated Parmesan cheese.

Louisiana Prawns Fettuccine

Serves 4

4 tbsp olive oil

450 g/1 lb raw tiger prawns, washed and peeled, shells and heads reserved

2 shallots, peeled and finely chopped

4 garlic cloves, peeled and finely chopped

large handful fresh basil leaves

1 carrot, peeled and finely chopped

1 onion, peeled and finely chopped

1 celery stick, trimmed and finely chopped

2–3 sprigs fresh parsley

2–3 sprigs fresh thyme

salt and freshly ground black pepper

pinch cayenne pepper

175 ml/6 fl oz dry white wine

450 g/1 lb ripe tomatoes, roughly chopped

juice of ½ lemon, or to taste

350 g/12 oz fettuccine

Heat 2 tablespoons of the olive oil in a large saucepan and add the reserved prawn shells and heads. Fry over a high heat for 2–3 minutes, until the shells turn pink and are lightly browned. Add half the shallots, half the garlic, half the basil, and the carrot, onion, celery, parsley and thyme. Season lightly with salt, pepper and cayenne and sauté for 2–3 minutes, stirring often. Pour in the wine and stir, scraping the pan well. Bring to the boil and simmer for 1 minute, then add the tomatoes. Cook for a further 3–4 minutes then pour in 200 ml/7 fl oz water. Bring to the boil, lower the heat and simmer for about 30 minutes, stirring often and mashing the prawn shells in order to release as much flavour as possible. Lower the heat if the sauce is reducing quickly. Strain through a sieve, pressing well to extract as much liquid as possible; there should be about 450 ml/¾ pint. Pour the liquid into a clean pan and bring to the boil, then lower the heat and simmer gently until the liquid is reduced by about half.

Heat the remaining olive oil over a high heat in a clean frying pan and add the peeled prawns. Season lightly and add the lemon juice. Cook for 1 minute, lower the heat and add the remaining shallots and garlic. Cook for 1 minute. Add the sauce and adjust the seasoning. Meanwhile, bring a large pan of lightly salted water to a rolling boil and add the fettuccine. Cook according to the packet instructions, or until *al dente*, and drain thoroughly. Transfer to a warmed serving dish. Add the sauce and toss well. Garnish with the remaining basil and serve immediately.

Salmon & Roasted Red Pepper Pasta

Serves 6

225 g/8 oz skinless and boneless
salmon fillet, thinly sliced
3 shallots, peeled and finely
chopped
1 tbsp freshly chopped parsley
6 tbsp olive oil
juice of $1/2$ lemon
2 red peppers, deseeded
and quartered
handful fresh basil leaves,
shredded
50 g/2 oz fresh breadcrumbs
4 tbsp extra virgin olive oil
450 g/1 lb fettuccine or linguine
6 spring onions, trimmed
and shredded
salt and freshly ground
black pepper

Preheat the grill to high. Place the salmon in a bowl. Add the shallots, parsley, 3 tablespoons of the olive oil and the lemon juice. Reserve.

Brush the pepper quarters with a little olive oil. Cook them under the preheated grill for 8–10 minutes, or until the skins have blackened and the flesh is tender. Place the peppers in a plastic bag until cool enough to handle. When cooled, peel the peppers and cut into strips. Put the strips into a bowl with the basil and the remaining olive oil and reserve.

Toast the breadcrumbs until dry and lightly browned then toss with the extra virgin olive oil and reserve.

Bring a large pan of salted water to a rolling boil and add the pasta. Cook according to the packet instructions, or until *al dente*.

Meanwhile, transfer the peppers and their marinade to a hot frying pan. Add the spring onions and cook for 1–2 minutes, or until they have just softened. Add the salmon and its marinade and cook for a further 1–2 minutes, or until the salmon is just cooked. Season to taste.

Drain the pasta thoroughly and transfer to a warmed serving bowl. Add the salmon mixture and toss gently. Garnish with the breadcrumbs and serve immediately.

Spaghettini with Peas, Spring Onions & Mint

Serves 6

pinch saffron strands
700 g/1½ lb fresh peas or
350 g/12 oz frozen petit
pois, thawed
75 g/3 oz unsalted butter, softened
6 spring onions, trimmed and
finely sliced
salt and freshly ground
black pepper
1 garlic clove, peeled and
finely chopped
2 tbsp freshly chopped mint
1 tbsp freshly snipped chives
450 g/1 lb spaghettini
freshly grated Parmesan cheese,
to serve

Soak the saffron in 2 tablespoons hot water while you prepare the sauce. Shell the peas if using fresh ones.

Heat 50 g/2 oz of the butter in a medium frying pan, add the spring onions and a little salt and cook over a low heat for 2–3 minutes, or until the onions are softened. Add the garlic, then the peas and 100 ml/3½ fl oz water. Bring to the boil and cook for 5–6 minutes, or until the peas are just tender. Stir in the mint and keep warm.

Blend the remaining butter and the saffron water in a large warmed serving bowl and reserve.

Meanwhile, bring a large pan of lightly salted water to a rolling boil and add the spaghettini. Cook according to the packet instructions, or until *al dente*.

Drain thoroughly, reserving 2–3 tablespoons of the pasta cooking water. Tip into a warmed serving bowl, add the pea sauce and toss together gently. Season to taste with salt and pepper. Serve immediately with extra black pepper and grated Parmesan cheese.

Fusilli with Spicy Tomato & Chorizo Sauce with Roasted Peppers

Serves 6

4 tbsp olive oil
1 red pepper, deseeded and quartered
1 yellow pepper, deseeded and quartered
175 g/6 oz chorizo (outer skin removed). roughly chopped
2 garlic cloves. peeled and finely chopped
large pinch chilli flakes
700 g/1 ½ lb ripe tomatoes, skinned and roughly chopped
salt and freshly ground black pepper
450 g/1 lb fusilli
basil leaves, to garnish
freshly grated Parmesan cheese, to serve

Preheat the grill to high. Brush the pepper quarters with 1 tablespoon of the olive oil, then cook under the preheated grill, turning once, for 8–10 minutes, or until the skins have blackened and the flesh is tender. Place the peppers in a plastic bag until cool enough to handle. When cooled, peel the peppers, slice very thinly and reserve.

Heat the remaining oil in a frying pan and add the chorizo. Cook over a medium heat for 3–4 minutes, or until starting to brown. Add the garlic and chilli flakes and cook for a further 2–3 minutes.

Add the tomatoes, season lightly with salt and pepper then cook gently for about 5 minutes, or until the tomatoes have broken down. Lower the heat and cook for a further 10–15 minutes, or until the sauce has thickened. Add the peppers and heat gently for 1–2 minutes. Adjust the seasoning to taste.

Meanwhile, bring a large pan of lightly salted water to a rolling boil. Add the fusilli and cook according to the packet instructions, or until *al dente*. Drain thoroughly and transfer to a warmed serving dish. Pour over the sauce, sprinkle with basil and serve with Parmesan cheese.

Pasta with Walnut Sauce

Serves 4

50 g/2 oz walnuts, toasted
3 spring onions, trimmed
and chopped
2 garlic cloves, peeled and sliced
1 tbsp freshly chopped parsley
or basil
5 tbsp extra virgin olive oil
salt and freshly ground
black pepper
450 g/1 lb broccoli, cut into florets
350 g/12 oz pasta shapes
1 red chilli, deseeded and
finely chopped

Place the toasted walnuts in a blender or food processor with the chopped spring onions, one of the garlic cloves and parsley or basil. Blend to a fairly smooth paste, then gradually add 3 tablespoons of the olive oil, until it is well mixed into the paste. Season the walnut paste to taste with salt and pepper and reserve.

Bring a large pan of lightly salted water to a rolling boil. Add the broccoli, return to the boil and cook for 2 minutes. Remove the broccoli, using a slotted draining spoon and refresh under cold running water. Drain again and pat dry on absorbent kitchen paper.

Bring the water back to a rolling boil. Add the pasta and cook according to the packet instructions, or until *al dente*.

Meanwhile, heat the remaining oil in a frying pan. Add the remaining garlic and chilli. Cook gently for 2 minutes, or until softened. Add the broccoli and walnut paste. Cook for a further 3–4 minutes, or until heated through.

Drain the pasta thoroughly and transfer to a large warmed serving bowl. Pour over the walnut and broccoli sauce. Toss together, adjust the seasoning and serve immediately.

Pasta Bean Soup

Serves 4–6

3 tbsp olive oil
2 celery sticks, trimmed and
finely chopped
100 g/3½ oz prosciutto or prosciutto
di speck, cut in pieces
1 red chilli, deseeded and
finely chopped
2 large potatoes, peeled and cut into
2.5 cm/1 in cubes
2 garlic cloves, peeled and
finely chopped
3 ripe plum tomatoes, skinned
and chopped
1 x 400 g can borlotti beans, drained
and rinsed
1 litre/1¾ pints chicken or
vegetable stock
100 g/3½ oz pasta shapes
large handful basil leaves, torn
salt and freshly ground
black pepper
shredded basil leaves, to garnish
crusty bread, to serve

Heat the olive oil in a heavy-based pan, add the celery and prosciutto and cook gently for 6–8 minutes, or until softened. Add the chopped chilli and potato cubes and cook for a further 10 minutes.

Add the garlic to the chilli and potato mixture and cook for 1 minute. Add the chopped tomatoes and simmer for 5 minutes. Stir in two-thirds of the beans, then pour in the chicken or vegetable stock and bring to the boil.

Add the pasta shapes to the soup stock and return it to simmering point. Cook the pasta for about 10 minutes, or until *al dente*.

Meanwhile, place the remaining beans in a food processor or blender and blend together with enough of the soup stock to make a smooth, thinnish purée.

When the pasta is cooked, stir in the puréed beans with the torn basil. Season the soup to taste with salt and pepper. Ladle into warmed serving bowls, garnish with shredded basil and serve immediately with plenty of crusty bread.

Gnocchetti with Broccoli Bacon Sauce

Serves 6

450 g/1 lb broccoli florets
4 tbsp olive oil
50 g/2 oz pancetta or smoked
bacon, finely chopped
1 small onion, peeled and
finely chopped
3 garlic cloves, peeled and sliced
200 ml/7 fl oz milk
450 g/1 lb gnocchetti
(little elongated ribbed shells)
50 g/2 oz freshly grated Parmesan
cheese, plus extra to serve
salt and freshly ground
black pepper

Bring a large pan of salted water to the boil. Add the broccoli florets and cook for about 8–10 minutes, or until very soft. Drain thoroughly, allow to cool slightly then chop finely and reserve.

Heat the olive oil in a heavy-based pan, add the pancetta or bacon and cook over a medium heat for 5 minutes, or until golden and crisp. Add the onion and cook for a further 5 minutes, or until soft and lightly golden. Add the garlic and cook for 1 minute.

Transfer the chopped broccoli to the bacon or pancetta mixture and pour in the milk. Bring slowly to the boil and simmer rapidly for about 15 minutes, or until reduced to a creamy texture.

Meanwhile, bring a large pan of lightly salted water to a rolling boil. Add the pasta and cook according to the packet instructions, or until *al dente*.

Drain the pasta thoroughly, reserving a little of the cooking water. Add the pasta and the Parmesan cheese to the broccoli mixture. Toss, adding enough of the reserved cooking water to make a creamy sauce. Season to taste with salt and pepper. Serve immediately with extra Parmesan cheese.

Penne with Artichokes, Bacon Mushrooms

Serves 6

2 tbsp olive oil
75 g/3 oz smoked bacon or
pancetta, chopped
1 small onion, peeled and
finely sliced
125 g/4 oz chestnut mushrooms,
wiped and sliced
2 garlic cloves, peeled and
finely chopped
400 g/14 oz can artichoke hearts,
drained and halved or quartered
if large
100 ml/3¹/₂ fl oz dry white wine
100 ml/3¹/₂ fl oz chicken stock
3 tbsp double cream
50 g/2 oz freshly grated Parmesan
cheese, plus extra to serve
salt and freshly ground
black pepper
450 g/1 lb penne
shredded basil leaves, to garnish

Heat the olive oil in a frying pan and add the pancetta or bacon and the onion. Cook over a medium heat for 8–10 minutes, or until the bacon is crisp and the onion is just golden. Add the mushrooms and garlic and cook for a further 5 minutes, or until softened.

Add the artichoke hearts to the mushroom mixture and cook for 3–4 minutes. Pour in the wine, bring to the boil then simmer rapidly until the liquid is reduced and syrupy.

Pour in the chicken stock, bring to the boil then simmer rapidly for about 5 minutes, or until slightly reduced. Reduce the heat slightly, then slowly stir in the double cream and Parmesan cheese. Season the sauce to taste with salt and pepper.

Meanwhile, bring a large pan of lightly salted water to a rolling boil. Add the pasta and cook according to the packet instructions, or until *al dente*.

Drain the pasta thoroughly and transfer to a large warmed serving dish. Pour over the sauce and toss together. Garnish with shredded basil and serve with extra Parmesan cheese.

Tagliarini with Broad Beans, Saffron & Crème Fraîche

Serves 2–3

225 g/8 oz fresh young broad
beans in pods or 100 g/3½ oz
frozen broad beans, thawed
1 tbsp olive oil
1 garlic clove, peeled and chopped
small handful basil leaves,
shredded
200 ml/7 fl oz crème fraîche
large pinch saffron strands
350 g/12 oz tagliarini
salt and freshly ground
black pepper
1 tbsp freshly snipped chives
freshly grated Parmesan cheese,
to serve

If using fresh broad beans, bring a pan of lightly salted water to the boil. Pod the beans and drop them into the boiling water for 1 minute. Drain and refresh under cold water. Drain again. Remove the outer skin of the beans and discard. If using thawed frozen broad beans, remove and discard the skins. Reserve the peeled beans.

Heat the olive oil in a saucepan. Add the peeled broad beans and the garlic and cook gently for 2–3 minutes. Stir in the basil, the crème fraîche and the pinch of saffron strands and simmer for 1 minute.

Meanwhile, bring a large pan of lightly salted water to a rolling boil. Add the pasta and cook according to the packet instructions, or until *al dente*. Drain the pasta well and add to the sauce. Toss together and season to taste with salt and pepper.

Transfer the pasta and sauce to a warmed serving dish. Sprinkle with snipped chives and serve immediately with Parmesan cheese.

Fish & Shellfish

There are so many delicious varieties of fish and shellfish that can be coupled with a myriad of pasta types to create stunning combinations of flavour and texture. If you are after a moreish taste and delicate texture, try the Pappardelle with Smoked Haddock & Blue Cheese Sauce, or for satisfying comfort food at its best opt for Crispy Cod Cannelloni.

Pappardelle with Smoked Haddock & Blue Cheese Sauce

Serves 4

350 g/12 oz smoked haddock
2 bay leaves
300 ml/ $^1/_2$ pint milk
400 g/14 oz pappardelle or tagliatelle
25 g/1 oz butter
25 g/1 oz plain flour
150 ml/ $^1/_4$ pint single cream or extra milk
125 g/4 oz Dolcelatte cheese or Gorgonzola, cut into small pieces
$^1/_4$ tsp freshly grated nutmeg
salt and freshly ground black pepper
40 g/1 $^1/_2$ oz toasted walnuts, chopped
1 tbsp freshly chopped parsley

Place the smoked haddock in a saucepan with 1 bay leaf and pour in the milk. Bring to the boil slowly, cover and simmer for 6–7 minutes, or until the fish is opaque. Remove and roughly flake the fish, discarding the skin and any bones. Strain the milk and reserve.

Bring a large pan of lightly salted water to a rolling boil. Add the pasta and cook according to the packet instructions, or until *al dente*.

Meanwhile, place the butter, flour and single cream, or milk if preferred, in a pan and stir to mix. Stir in the reserved warm milk and add the remaining bay leaf. Bring to the boil, whisking all the time until smooth and thick. Gently simmer for 3–4 minutes, stirring frequently. Discard the bay leaf.

Add the Dolcelatte or Gorgonzola cheese to the sauce. Heat gently, stirring until melted. Add the flaked haddock and season to taste with nutmeg and salt and pepper.

Drain the pasta thoroughly and return to the pan. Add the sauce and toss gently to coat, taking care not to break up the flakes of fish. Tip into a warmed serving bowl, sprinkle with toasted walnuts and parsley and serve immediately.

Special Seafood Lasagne

Serves 4–6

450 g/1 lb fresh haddock
fillet, skinned
150 ml/ ¼ pint dry white wine
150 ml/ ¼ pint fish stock
½ onion, peeled and thickly sliced
1 bay leaf
75 g/3 oz butter
350 g/12 oz leeks, trimmed and
thickly sliced
1 garlic clove, peeled and crushed
25 g/1 oz plain flour
150 ml/ ¼ pint single cream
2 tbsp freshly chopped dill
salt and freshly ground
black pepper
8–12 sheets dried lasagne
verde, cooked
225 g/8 oz ready-cooked
seafood cocktail
50 g/2 oz Gruyère cheese, grated

Preheat the oven to 200°C/400°F/Gas Mark 6, 15 minutes before cooking. Place the haddock in a pan with the wine, fish stock, onion and bay leaf. Bring to the boil slowly, cover and simmer gently for 5 minutes, or until the fish is opaque. Remove and flake the fish, discarding any bones. Strain the cooking juices and reserve.

Melt 50 g/2 oz of the butter in a large saucepan. Add the leeks and garlic and cook gently for 10 minutes. Remove from the pan, using a slotted draining spoon, and reserve.

Melt the remaining butter in a small saucepan. Stir in the flour, then gradually whisk in the cream, off the heat, followed by the reserved cooking juices. Bring to the boil slowly, whisking until thickened. Stir in the dill and season to taste with salt and pepper.

Spoon a little of the sauce into the base of a buttered 2.8 litre/5 pint shallow oven-proof dish. Top with a layer of lasagne, followed by the haddock, seafood cocktail and leeks. Spoon over enough sauce to cover. Continue layering up, finishing with sheets of lasagne topped with sauce.

Sprinkle over the grated Gruyère cheese and bake in the preheated oven for 40–45 minutes, or until golden-brown and bubbling. Serve immediately on warmed plates.

Saucy Cod Pasta Bake

Serves 4

450 g/1 lb cod fillets, skinned
2 tbsp sunflower oil
1 onion, peeled and chopped
4 rashers smoked streaky bacon,
rind removed and chopped
150 g/5 oz baby button
mushrooms, wiped
2 celery sticks, trimmed and
thinly sliced
2 small courgettes, halved
lengthwise and sliced
400 g can chopped tomatoes
100 ml/3^1/$_2$ fl oz fish stock or dry
white wine
1 tbsp freshly chopped tarragon
salt and freshly ground black pepper

For the pasta topping:

225–275 g/8–10 oz pasta shells
25 g/1 oz butter
4 tbsp plain flour
450 ml/ ^{3}/$_4$ pint milk

Preheat the oven to 200°C/400°F/Gas Mark 6, 15 minutes before cooking. Cut the cod into bite-sized pieces and reserve.

Heat the sunflower oil in a large saucepan, add the onion and bacon and cook for 7–8 minutes. Add the mushrooms and celery and cook for 5 minutes, or until fairly soft.

Add the courgettes and tomatoes to the bacon mixture and pour in the fish stock or wine. Bring to the boil, then simmer uncovered for 5 minutes, or until the sauce has thickened slightly. Remove from the heat and stir in the cod pieces and the tarragon. Season to taste with salt and pepper, then spoon into a large oiled baking dish.

Meanwhile, bring a large pan of lightly salted water to a rolling boil. Add the pasta shells and cook, according to the packet instructions, or until *al dente*.

For the topping, place the butter and flour in a saucepan and pour in the milk. Bring to the boil slowly, whisking until thickened and smooth.

Drain the pasta thoroughly, and stir into the sauce. Spoon carefully over the fish and vegetables. Place in the preheated oven and bake for 20–25 minutes, or until the top is lightly browned and bubbling.

Pasta Provençale

Serves 4

2 tbsp olive oil
1 garlic clove, peeled and crushed
1 onion, peeled and finely chopped
1 small fennel bulb, trimmed and
halved and thinly sliced
400 g can chopped tomatoes
1 rosemary sprig, plus extra
sprig to garnish
350 g/12 oz monkfish, skinned
2 tsp lemon juice
400 g/14 oz gnocchi pasta
50 g/2 oz pitted black olives
200 g can flageolet beans, drained
and rinsed
1 tbsp freshly chopped oregano,
plus sprig to garnish
salt and freshly ground
black pepper

Heat the olive oil in a large saucepan, add the garlic and onion and cook gently for 5 minutes. Add the fennel and cook for a further 5 minutes. Stir in the chopped tomatoes and rosemary sprig. Half-cover the pan and simmer for 10 minutes.

Cut the monkfish into bite-sized pieces and sprinkle with the lemon juice. Add to the tomatoes, cover and simmer gently for 5 minutes, or until the fish is opaque.

Meanwhile, bring a large pan of lightly salted water to a rolling boil. Add the pasta and cook according to the packet instructions, or until *al dente*. Drain the pasta thoroughly and return to the saucepan.

Remove the rosemary from the tomato sauce. Stir in the black olives, flageolet beans and chopped oregano, then season to taste with salt and pepper. Add the sauce to the pasta and toss gently together to coat, taking care not to break up the monkfish. Tip into a warmed serving bowl. Garnish with rosemary and oregano sprigs and serve immediately.

Seared Salmon Lemon Linguine

Serves 4

4 small skinless salmon fillets,
each about 75 g/3 oz
2 tsp sunflower oil
$1/2$ tsp mixed or black
peppercorns, crushed
400 g/14 oz linguine
15 g/ $1/2$ oz unsalted butter
1 bunch spring onions, trimmed
and shredded
300 ml/ $1/2$ pint soured cream
zest of 1 lemon, finely grated
50 g/2 oz freshly grated
Parmesan cheese
1 tbsp lemon juice
pinch of salt

To garnish:

dill sprigs
lemon slices

Brush the salmon fillets with the sunflower oil, sprinkle with crushed peppercorns and press on firmly and reserve.

Bring a large pan of lightly salted water to a rolling boil. Add the linguine and cook according to the packet instructions, or until *al dente*.

Meanwhile, melt the butter in a saucepan and cook the shredded spring onions gently for 2–3 minutes, or until soft. Stir in the soured cream and the lemon zest and remove from the heat. If you are unable to find soured cream, stir 1 teaspoon lemon juice into 300 ml/$1/2$ pint of double cream and leave at room temperature for 20 minutes before using.

Preheat a griddle or heavy-based frying pan until very hot. Add the salmon and sear for $1^1/2$–2 minutes on each side. Remove from the pan and allow to cool slightly.

Bring the soured cream sauce to the boil and stir in the Parmesan cheese and lemon juice. Drain the pasta thoroughly and return to the pan. Pour over the sauce and toss gently to coat.

Spoon the pasta on to warmed serving plates and top with the salmon fillets. Serve immediately with sprigs of dill and lemon slices.

Tagliatelle with Tuna & Anchovy Tapenade

Serves 4

400 g/14 oz tagliatelle
125 g can tuna fish in oil, drained
45 g/1³/₄ oz can anchovy
fillets, drained
150 g/5 oz pitted black olives
2 tbsp capers in brine, drained
2 tsp lemon juice
100 ml/3¹/₂ fl oz olive oil
2 tbsp freshly chopped parsley
freshly ground black pepper
sprigs of flat-leaf parsley, to garnish

Bring a large pan of lightly salted water to a rolling boil. Add the tagliatelle and cook according to the packet instructions, or until *al dente*.

Meanwhile, place the tuna fish, anchovy fillets, olives and capers in a food processor with the lemon juice and 2 tablespoons of the olive oil and blend for a few seconds until roughly chopped.

With the motor running, pour in the remaining olive oil in a steady stream; the resulting mixture should be slightly chunky rather than smooth.

Spoon the sauce into a bowl, stir in the chopped parsley and season to taste with black pepper. Check the taste of the sauce and add a little more lemon juice, if required.

Drain the pasta thoroughly. Pour the sauce into the pan and cook over a low heat for 1–2 minutes to warm through.

Return the drained pasta to the pan and mix together with the sauce. Tip into a warmed serving bowl or spoon on to warm individual plates. Garnish with sprigs of flat-leaf parsley and serve immediately.

Pan-fried Scallops Pasta

Serves 4

16 large scallops, shelled
1 tbsp olive oil
1 garlic clove, peeled and crushed
1 tsp freshly chopped thyme
400 g/14 oz penne
4 sun-dried tomatoes in oil, drained
and thinly sliced
thyme or oregano sprigs, to garnish

For the tomato dressing:

2 sun-dried tomatoes in oil, drained
and chopped
1 tbsp red wine vinegar
2 tsp balsamic vinegar
1 tsp sun-dried tomato paste
1 tsp caster sugar
salt and freshly ground
black pepper
2 tbsp oil from a jar of
sun-dried tomatoes
2 tbsp olive oil

Rinse the scallops and pat dry on absorbent kitchen paper. Place in a bowl and add the olive oil, crushed garlic and thyme. Cover and chill in the refrigerator until ready to cook.

Bring a large pan of lightly salted water to a rolling boil. Add the penne and cook according to the packet instructions, or until *al dente*.

Meanwhile, make the dressing. Place the sun-dried tomatoes into a small bowl or glass jar and add the vinegars, tomato paste, sugar, salt and pepper. Whisk well, then pour into a food processor.

With the motor running, pour in the sun-dried tomato oil and olive oil in a steady stream to make a thick, smooth dressing.

Preheat a large, dry cast-iron griddle pan over a high heat for about 5 minutes. Lower the heat to medium then add the scallops to the pan. Cook for 1½ minutes on each side. Remove from the pan.

Drain the pasta thoroughly and return to the pan. Add the sliced sun-dried tomatoes and dressing and toss. Divide between individual serving plates, top each portion with 4 scallops, garnish with fresh thyme or oregano sprigs and serve immediately.

Smoked Mackerel & Pasta Frittata

Serves 4

25 g/1 oz tricolore pasta spirals
or shells
225 g/8 oz smoked mackerel
6 medium eggs
3 tbsp milk
2 tsp wholegrain mustard
2 tbsp freshly chopped parsley
salt and freshly ground
black pepper
25 g/1 oz unsalted butter
6 spring onions, trimmed and
diagonally sliced
50 g/2 oz frozen peas, thawed
75 g/3 oz mature Cheddar
cheese, grated

To serve:

green salad
warm crusty bread

Preheat the grill to high just before cooking. Bring a pan of lightly salted water to a rolling boil. Add the pasta and cook according to the packet instructions, or until *al dente*. Drain thoroughly and reserve.

Remove the skin from the mackerel and break the fish into large flakes, discarding any bones, and reserve.

Place the eggs, milk, mustard and parsley in a bowl and whisk together. Season with just a little salt and plenty of freshly ground black pepper and reserve.

Melt the butter in a large, heavy-based frying pan. Cook the spring onions gently for 3–4 minutes, until soft. Pour in the egg mixture, then add the drained pasta, peas and half of the mackerel.

Gently stir the mixture in the pan for 1–2 minutes, or until beginning to set. Stop stirring and cook for about 1 minute until the underneath is golden-brown.

Scatter the remaining mackerel over the frittata, followed by the grated cheese. Place under the preheated grill for about 1^1/$_2$ minutes, or until golden-brown and set. Cut into wedges and serve immediately with salad and crusty bread.

Crispy Cod Cannelloni

Serves 4

1 tbsp olive oil
8 dried cannelloni tubes
25 g/1 oz unsalted butter
225 g/8 oz button mushrooms,
thinly sliced
175 g/6 oz leeks, trimmed and
finely chopped
175 g/6 oz cod, skinned
and diced
175 g/6 oz cream cheese
salt and freshly ground
black pepper
15 g/ ½ oz Parmesan
cheese, grated
50 g/2 oz fine fresh white
breadcrumbs
3 tbsp plain flour
1 medium egg, lightly beaten
oil for deep frying
fresh herbs or salad leaves,
to serve

Add 1 teaspoon of the olive oil to a large pan of lightly salted water and bring to a rolling boil. Add the cannelloni tubes and cook, uncovered, for 5 minutes. Drain and leave in a bowl of cold water.

Melt the butter with the remaining oil in a saucepan. Add the mushrooms and leeks and cook gently for 5 minutes. Turn up the heat and cook for 1–2 minutes, or until the mixture is fairly dry. Add the cod and cook, stirring, for 2–3 minutes, or until the fish is opaque. Add the cream cheese to the pan and stir until melted. Season to taste with salt and pepper, then leave the cod mixture to cool.

Drain the cannelloni. Using a piping bag without a nozzle, or a spoon, fill the cannelloni with the cod mixture.

Mix the Parmesan cheese and breadcrumbs together on a plate. Dip the filled cannelloni into the flour, then into the beaten egg and finally into the breadcrumb mixture. Dip the ends twice to ensure they are thoroughly coated. Chill in the refrigerator for 30 minutes.

Heat the oil for deep frying to 180°C/350°F. Fry the stuffed cannelloni in batches for 2–3 minutes, or until the coating is crisp and golden-brown. Drain on absorbent kitchen paper and serve immediately with fresh herbs or salad leaves.

Spaghetti alle Vongole

Serves 4

1.8 kg/4 lb small fresh clams
6 tbsp dry white wine
2 tbsp olive oil
1 small onion, peeled and
finely chopped
2 garlic cloves, peeled
and crushed
400 g/14 oz spaghetti
2 tbsp freshly chopped parsley
2 tbsp freshly chopped or
torn basil
salt and freshly ground
black pepper
oregano leaves, to garnish

Soak the clams in lightly salted cold water for 8 hours before required, changing the water once or twice. Scrub the clams, removing any that have broken shells or that remain open when tapped. Place the prepared clams in a large saucepan and pour in the wine. Cover with a tight-fitting lid and cook over a medium heat for 5–6 minutes, shaking the pan occasionally, until the shells have opened. Strain the clams and cooking juices through a sieve lined with muslin and reserve. Discard any clams that have remained unopened.

Heat the olive oil in a saucepan and fry the onion and garlic gently for 10 minutes, or until very soft.

Meanwhile, bring a large pan of lightly salted water to a rolling boil. Add the pasta and cook according to the packet instructions, or until *al dente*.

Add the cooked clams to the onions and garlic and pour in the reserved cooking juices. Bring to the boil, then add the parsley and basil and season to taste with salt and black pepper.

Drain the spaghetti thoroughly. Return to the pan and add the clams with their sauce. Toss together gently, then tip into a large warmed serving bowl or into individual bowls. Serve immediately, sprinkled with oregano leaves.

Seafood Parcels with Pappardelle & Coriander Pesto

Serves 4

300 g/11 oz pappardelle
or tagliatelle
8 raw tiger prawns, shelled
12 raw queen scallops
225 g/8oz baby squid, cleaned
and cut into rings
4 tbsp dry white wine
4 thin slices of lemon

Coriander pesto:

50 g/2 oz fresh coriander leaves
1 garlic clove, peeled
25 g/1 oz pine nuts, toasted
1 tsp lemon juice
5 tbsp olive oil
1 tbsp grated Parmesan cheese
salt and freshly ground
black pepper

Preheat the oven to 180°C/350°F/Gas Mark 4, 10 minutes before cooking. To make the pesto, blend the coriander leaves, garlic, pine nuts and lemon juice with 1 tablespoon of the olive oil to a smooth paste in a food processor. With the motor running slowly add the remaining oil. Stir the Parmesan cheese into the pesto and season to taste with salt and pepper.

Bring a pan of lightly salted water to a rolling boil. Add the pasta and cook for 3 minutes only. Drain thoroughly, return to the pan and spoon over two-thirds of the pesto. Toss to coat.

Cut out 4 circles, about 30 cm/12 in in diameter, from non-stick baking parchment. Spoon the pasta on to one half of each circle. Top each pile of pasta with 2 prawns, 3 scallops and a few squid rings. Spoon 1 tablespoon of wine over each serving, then drizzle with the remaining coriander pesto and top with a slice of lemon.

Close the parcels by folding over the other half of the paper, to make a semi-circle, then turn and twist the edges of the paper to secure.

Place the parcels on a baking tray and bake in the preheated oven for 15 minutes, or until cooked. Serve the parcels immediately, allowing each person to open their own.

Pasta & Mussels in Tomato & Wine Sauce

Serves 4

900 g/2 lb fresh live mussels
1 bay leaf
150 ml/¹/₄ pint light red wine
15 g/¹/₂ oz unsalted butter
1 tbsp olive oil
1 red onion, peeled and thinly sliced
2 garlic cloves, peeled and crushed
550 g/1 ¹/₄ lb ripe tomatoes, skinned, deseeded and chopped
400 g/14 oz fiochetti or penne
3 tbsp freshly chopped or torn basil
salt and freshly ground black pepper
basil leaves, to garnish
crusty bread, to serve

Scrub the mussels and remove any beards. Discard any that do not close when lightly tapped. Place in a large pan with the bay leaf and pour in the wine. Cover with a tight-fitting lid and steam, shaking the pan occasionally, for 3–4 minutes, or until the mussels open. Remove the mussels with a slotted spoon, discarding any that have not opened, and reserve. Strain the cooking liquid through a muslin-lined sieve and reserve.

Melt the butter with the oil in a large saucepan and gently cook the onion and garlic for 10 minutes, until soft. Add the reserved cooking liquid and the tomatoes and simmer, uncovered, for 6–7 minutes, or until very soft and the sauce has reduced slightly.

Meanwhile, bring a large pan of lightly salted water to a rolling boil. Add the pasta and cook acording to the packet instructions, or until *al dente*.

Drain the pasta thoroughly and return to the pan. Add the mussels, removing the shells if you prefer, with the tomato sauce. Stir in the basil and season to taste with salt and pepper. Toss together gently. Tip into warmed serving bowls, garnish with fresh basil leaves and serve with crusty bread.

Salmon & Spaghetti in a Creamy Egg Sauce

Serves 4

3 medium eggs
1 tbsp freshly chopped parsley
1 tbsp freshly chopped dill
40 g/1¹/₂ oz freshly grated
Parmesan cheese
40 g/1¹/₂ oz freshly grated
pecorino cheese
2 tbsp dry white wine
freshly ground black pepper
400 g/14 oz spaghetti
350 g/12 oz salmon fillet, skinned
25 g/1 oz butter
1 tsp olive oil
flat leaf parsley sprigs, to garnish

Beat the eggs in a bowl with the parsley, dill, half of the Parmesan and pecorino cheeses and the white wine. Season to taste with freshly ground black pepper and reserve.

Bring a large pan of lightly salted water to a rolling boil. Add the spaghetti and cook according to the packet instructions, or until *al dente*.

Meanwhile, cut the salmon into bite-sized pieces. Melt the butter in a large frying pan with the oil and cook the salmon pieces for 3–4 minutes, or until opaque.

Drain the spaghetti thoroughly, return to the pan and immediately add the egg mixture. Remove from the heat and toss well; the eggs will cook in the heat of the spaghetti to make a creamy sauce.

Stir in the remaining cheeses and the cooked pieces of salmon and toss again. Tip into a warmed serving bowl or on to individual plates. Garnish with sprigs of flat leaf parsley.

Creamy Coconut Seafood Pasta

Serves 4

400 g/14 oz egg tagliatelle
1 tsp sunflower oil
1 tsp sesame oil
4 spring onions, trimmed and
sliced diagonally
1 garlic clove, peeled and crushed
1 red chilli, deseeded and
finely chopped
2.5 cm/1 inch piece fresh root ginger,
peeled and grated
150 ml/ $^1/_4$ pint coconut milk
100 ml/3$^1/_2$ fl oz double cream
225 g/8 oz cooked peeled
tiger prawns
185 g/6$^1/_2$ oz fresh white crab meat
2 tbsp freshly chopped coriander,
plus sprigs to garnish
salt and freshly ground
black pepper

Bring a large pan of lightly salted water to a rolling boil. Add the pasta and cook according to the packet instructions, or until *al dente*.

Meanwhile, heat the sunflower and sesame oils together in a saucepan. Add the spring onions, garlic, chilli and ginger and cook for 3–4 minutes, or until softened.

Blend the coconut milk and cream together in a jug. Add the prawns and crab meat to the pan and stir over a low heat for a few seconds to heat through. Gradually pour in the coconut cream, stirring all the time.

Stir the chopped coriander into the seafood sauce and season to taste with salt and pepper. Continue heating the sauce gently until piping hot, but do not allow to boil.

Drain the pasta thoroughly and return to the pan. Add the seafood sauce and gently toss together to coat the pasta. Tip into a warmed serving dish or spoon on to individual plates. Serve immediately, garnished with fresh coriander sprigs.

Fettuccine with Sardines & Spinach

Serves 4

120g can sardines in olive oil
400 g/14 oz fettuccine or tagliarini
40 g/1 ^{1}/$_2$ oz butter
2 tbsp olive oil
50 g/2 oz one-day-old
white breadcrumbs
1 garlic clove, peeled and
finely chopped
50 g/2 oz pine nuts
125 g/4 oz chestnut mushrooms,
wiped and sliced
125 g/4 oz baby spinach
leaves, rinsed
150 ml/ ^{1}/$_4$ pint crème fraîche
rind of 1 lemon, finely grated
salt and freshly ground
black pepper

Drain the sardines and cut in half lengthwise. Remove the bones, then cut the fish into 2.5 cm/1 inch pieces and reserve.

Bring a large pan of lightly salted water to a rolling boil. Add the pasta and cook according to the packet instructions, or until *al dente*.

Meanwhile, melt half the butter with the olive oil in a large saucepan, add the breadcrumbs and fry, stirring, until they begin to turn crisp. Add the garlic and pine nuts and continue to cook until golden-brown. Remove from the pan and reserve. Wipe the pan clean.

Melt the remaining butter in the pan, add the mushrooms and cook for 4–5 minutes, or until soft. Add the spinach and cook, stirring, for 1 minute, or until beginning to wilt. Stir in the crème fraîche and lemon rind and bring to the boil. Simmer gently until the spinach is just cooked. Season the sauce to taste with salt and pepper.

Drain the pasta thoroughly and return to the pan. Add the spinach sauce and sardine pieces and gently toss together. Tip into a warmed serving dish. Sprinkle with the toasted breadcrumbs and pine nut mixture and serve immediately.

Sweet-&-Sour Fish with Crispy Noodles

Serves 4

350 g/12 oz plaice fillets, skinned
3 tbsp plain flour
pinch of Chinese five spice powder
2.5 cm/1 inch piece fresh root ginger,
peeled and grated
4 spring onions, trimmed and
finely sliced
3 tbsp dry sherry
1 tbsp dark soy sauce
2 tsp soft light brown sugar
1 tsp rice or sherry vinegar
1 tsp chilli sauce
salt and freshly ground
black pepper
125 g/4 oz thin, transparent rice
noodles or rice sticks
oil for deep frying

To garnish:

spring onion tassels
slices of red chilli

Cut the plaice fillets into 5 cm/2 inch slices. Mix the flour with the five spice powder in a bowl. Add the fish, a few pieces at a time, and toss to coat thoroughly. Reserve.

Place the ginger, spring onions, sherry, soy sauce, sugar, vinegar and chilli sauce in a small saucepan and season lightly with salt and pepper. Heat gently until the sugar has dissolved, then bubble the sauce for 2–3 minutes.

Break the noodles into pieces about 7.5 cm/3 inch long. Heat the oil in a deep fryer to 180°C/350°F. Deep-fry small handfuls of noodles for about 30 seconds, until puffed up and crisp. Remove and drain on absorbent kitchen paper.

Deep-fry the plaice for 1–2 minutes, or until firm and cooked. Remove and drain on absorbent kitchen paper.

Place the cooked fish in a warmed serving bowl, drizzle over the sauce and garnish with spring onion tassels and slices of red chilli. Pile the noodles into another bowl and serve.

Warm Swordfish Niçoise

Serves 4

4 swordfish steaks, about 2.5 cm/
1 inch thick, weighing about
175 g/6 oz each
juice of 1 lime
2 tbsp olive oil
salt and freshly ground
black pepper
400 g/14 oz farfalle
225 g/8 oz French beans, topped
and cut in half
1 tsp Dijon mustard
2 tsp white wine vinegar
pinch caster sugar
3 tbsp olive oil
225 g/8 oz ripe tomatoes,
quartered
50 g/2 oz pitted black olives
2 medium eggs, hard boiled
and quartered
8 anchovy fillets, drained and cut
in half lengthways

Place the swordfish steaks in a shallow dish. Mix the lime juice with the oil, season to taste with salt and pepper and spoon over the steaks. Turn the steaks to coat them evenly. Cover and place in the refrigerator to marinate for 1 hour.

Bring a large pan of lightly salted water to a rolling boil. Add the farfalle and cook according to the packet instructions, or until *al dente*. Add the French beans about 4 minutes before the end of cooking time.

Mix the mustard, vinegar and sugar together in a small jug. Gradually whisk in the olive oil to make a thick dressing.

Cook the swordfish in a griddle pan or under a hot preheated grill for 2 minutes on each side, or until just cooked through; overcooking will make it tough and dry. Remove and cut into 2 cm/³/₄ inch chunks.

Drain the pasta and beans thoroughly and place in a large bowl. Pour over the dressing and toss to coat. Add the cooked swordfish, tomatoes, olives, hard-boiled eggs and anchovy fillets. Gently toss together, taking care not to break up the eggs.

Tip into a warmed serving bowl or divide the pasta between individual plates. Serve immediately.

Meat

With perfect combinations of deliciously savoury meats including lamb, beef and chorizo, and pastas such as tagliatelle, cannelloni, lasagne and rigatoni, choosing which recipe to cook next will be the hardest part for meat lovers! For something different, opt for the Moroccan Penne, or if it's classic flavours you're after, the Gnocchi & Parma Ham Bake is not to be missed.

Spaghetti Bolognese

Serves 4

3 tbsp olive oil
50 g/2 oz unsmoked streaky bacon,
rind removed and chopped
1 small onion, peeled and
finely chopped
1 carrot, peeled and finely chopped
1 celery, trimmed and finely chopped
2 garlic cloves, peeled and crushed
1 bay leaf
500 g/1 lb 2 oz minced beef steak
400 g can chopped tomatoes
2 tbsp tomato paste
150 ml/ ¼ pint red wine
150 ml/ ¼ pint beef stock
salt and freshly ground black pepper
450 g/1 lb spaghetti
freshly grated Parmesan cheese,
to serve

Heat the olive oil in a large heavy-based pan, add the bacon and cook gently for 5 minutes or until slightly coloured. Add the onion, carrot, celery, garlic and bay leaf and cook, stirring, for 8 minutes, or until the vegetables are soft.

Add the minced beef to the pan and cook, stirring with a wooden spoon to break up any lumps in the meat, for 5-8 minutes, or until browned.

Stir the tomatoes and tomato paste into the mince and pour in the wine and stock. Bring to the boil, lower the heat and simmer for a least 40 minutes, stirring occasionally. The longer you leave the sauce to cook, the more intense the flavour. Season to taste with salt and pepper and remove the bay leaf.

Meanwhile, bring a large pan of lightly salted water to a rolling boil, add the spaghetti and cook for about 8 minutes or until *al dente*. Drain and arrange on warmed serving plates. Top with the prepared Bolognese sauce and serve immediately sprinkled with grated Parmesan cheese.

Lasagne

Serves 4

75 g/3 oz butter
4 tbsp plain flour
750 ml/ $1/4$ pint milk
1 tsp wholegrain mustard
salt and freshly ground
black pepper
$1/4$ tsp freshly grated nutmeg
9 sheets lasagne
1 quantity of prepared Bolognese
sauce, *see* page 114
75 g/3 oz freshly grated
Parmesan cheese
freshly chopped parsley,
to garnish
garlic bread, to serve

Preheat the oven to 200°C/400°F/Gas Mark 6, 15 minutes before cooking. Melt the butter in a small heavy-based pan, add the flour and cook gently, stirring, for 2 minutes. Remove from the heat and gradually stir in the milk. Return to the heat and cook, stirring, for 2 minutes, or until the sauce thickens. Bring to the boil, remove from the heat and stir in the mustard. Season to taste with salt, pepper and nutmeg.

Butter a rectangular ovenproof dish and spread a thin layer of the white sauce over the base. Cover completely with 3 sheets of lasagne.

Spoon a quarter of the prepared Bolognese sauce over the lasagne. Spoon over a quarter of the remaining white sauce, then sprinkle with a quarter of the grated Parmesan cheese. Repeat the layers, finishing with Parmesan cheese.

Bake in the preheated oven for 30 minutes, or until golden-brown. Garnish with chopped parsley and serve immediately with warm garlic bread.

Cannelloni with Spicy Bolognese Filling

Serves 6

12 dried cannelloni tubes
300 ml/ ½ pint double cream
75 g/3 oz freshly grated
Parmesan cheese
¼ tsp freshly grated nutmeg
crisp green salad, to serve

For the filling:

2 tbsp olive oil
1 small onion, peeled and
finely chopped
2 garlic cloves, peeled and crushed
500 g/1 lb 2 oz minced beef steak
¼ tsp crushed chilli flakes
1 tsp fennel seeds
2 tbsp freshly chopped oregano
400 g can chopped tomatoes
1 tbsp sun-dried tomato paste
150 ml/ ¼ pint red wine
salt and freshly ground
black pepper

Preheat the oven to 200°C/400°F/Gas Mark 6, 15 minutes before cooking the stuffed cannelloni. To make the Bolognese sauce, heat the oil in a large heavy-based pan, add the onion and garlic and cook gently for 8 minutes, or until soft. Add the minced beef and cook, stirring with a wooden spoon to break up lumps, for 5–8 minutes, or until the meat is browned.

Stir in the chilli flakes, fennel seeds, oregano, tomatoes and tomato paste and pour in the wine. Season well with salt and pepper. Bring to the boil, cover and lower the heat, then simmer for at least 30 minutes, stirring occasionally. Remove the lid and simmer for a further 10 minutes. Allow to cool slightly.

Using a teaspoon, fill the cannelloni tubes with the meat filling. Lay the stuffed cannelloni side by side in a lightly oiled ovenproof dish.

Mix the double cream with three-quarters of the Parmesan cheese and the nutmeg. Pour over the cannelloni and sprinkle with the remaining cheese. Bake in the preheated oven for 30 minutes, or until golden-brown and bubbling. Serve immediately with a green salad.

Spaghetti Meatballs

Serves 4

400 g can chopped tomatoes
1 tbsp tomato paste
1 tsp chilli sauce
1/4 tsp brown sugar
salt and freshly ground
black pepper
350 g/12 oz spaghetti
75g/3 oz Cheddar cheese, grated,
plus extra to serve
freshly chopped parsley, to garnish

For the meatballs:

450 g/1 lb lean pork or beef mince
125 g/4 oz fresh breadcrumbs
1 large onion, peeled and
finely chopped
1 medium egg, beaten
1 tbsp tomato paste
2 tbsp freshly chopped parsley
1 tbsp freshly chopped oregano

Preheat the oven to 200°C/400°F/Gas Mark 6, 15 minutes before using. Place the chopped tomatoes, tomato paste, chilli sauce and sugar in a saucepan. Season to taste with salt and pepper and bring to the boil. Cover and simmer for 15 minutes, then cook, uncovered, for a further 10 minutes, or until the sauce has reduced and thickened.

Meanwhile, make the meatballs. Place the meat, breadcrumbs and onion in a food processor. Blend until all the ingredients are well mixed. Add the beaten egg, tomato paste, parsley and oregano and season to taste. Blend again.

Shape the mixture into small balls, about the size of an apricot, and place on an oiled baking tray. Cook in the preheated oven for 25–30 minutes, or until browned and cooked.

Meanwhile, bring a large pan of lightly salted water to a rolling boil. Add the pasta and cook according to the packet instructions, or until *al dente*.

Drain the pasta and return to the pan. Pour over the tomato sauce and toss gently to coat the spaghetti. Tip into a warmed serving dish and top with the meatballs. Garnish with chopped parsley and serve immediately with grated cheese.

Chorizo with Pasta in a Tomato Sauce

Serves 4

25 g/1 oz butter
2 tbsp olive oil
2 large onions, peeled and finely sliced
1 tsp soft brown sugar
2 garlic cloves, peeled and crushed
225 g/8 oz chorizo, sliced
1 chilli, deseeded and finely sliced
400g can chopped tomatoes
1 tbsp sun-dried tomato paste
150 ml/¹/₄ pint red wine
salt and freshly ground black pepper
450 g/1 lb rigatoni
freshly chopped parsley, to garnish

Melt the butter with the olive oil in a large heavy-based pan. Add the onions and sugar and cook over a very low heat, stirring occasionally, for 15 minutes, or until soft and starting to caramelise.

Add the garlic and chorizo to the pan and cook for 5 minutes. Stir in the chilli, chopped tomatoes and tomato paste, and pour in the wine. Season well with salt and pepper. Bring to the boil, cover, reduce the heat and simmer for 30 minutes, stirring occasionally. Remove the lid and simmer for a further 10 minutes, or until the sauce starts to thicken.

Meanwhile, bring a large pan of lightly salted water to the boil. Add the pasta and cook according to the packet instructions, or until *al dente*.

Drain the pasta, reserving 2 tablespoons of the water, and return to the pan. Add the chorizo sauce with the reserved cooking water and toss gently until the pasta is evenly covered. Tip into a warmed serving dish, sprinkle with the parsley and serve immediately.

Moroccan Penne

Serves 4

1 tbsp sunflower oil
1 red onion, peeled and chopped
2 cloves garlic, peeled and crushed
1 tbsp coriander seeds
$^1/_4$ tsp cumin seeds
$^1/_4$ tsp freshly grated nutmeg
450 g/1 lb lean lamb mince
1 aubergine, trimmed and diced
400 g can chopped tomatoes
300 ml/ $^1/_2$ pint vegetable stock
125 g/4 oz ready-to-eat
apricots, chopped
12 black olives, pitted
salt and freshly ground
black pepper
350 g/12 oz penne
1 tbsp toasted pine nuts, to garnish

Preheat the oven to 200°C/400°F/Gas Mark 6, 15 minutes before using. Heat the sunflower oil in a large flameproof casserole. Add the chopped onion and fry for 5 minutes, or until softened.

Using a pestle and mortar, pound the garlic, coriander seeds, cumin seeds and grated nutmeg together into a paste. Add to the onion and cook for 3 minutes.

Add the lamb mince to the casserole and fry, stirring with a wooden spoon, for 4–5 minutes, or until the mince has broken up and browned.

Add the aubergine to the mince and fry for 5 minutes. Stir in the chopped tomatoes and vegetable stock and bring to the boil. Add the apricots and olives, then season well with salt and pepper. Return to the boil, lower the heat and simmer for 15 minutes.

Add the penne to the casserole, stir well, then cover and place in the preheated oven. Cook for 10 minutes then stir and return to the oven, uncovered, for a further 15–20 minutes, or until the pasta is *al dente*. Remove from the oven, sprinkle with the toasted pine nuts and serve immediately.

Pasta Pork Ragù

1 tbsp sunflower oil
1 leek, trimmed and thinly sliced
225 g/8 oz pork fillet, diced
1 garlic clove, peeled and crushed
2 tsp paprika
$^{1}/_{4}$ tsp cayenne pepper
150 ml/ $^{1}/_{4}$ pint white wine
600 ml/1 pint vegetable stock
400g can borlotti beans, drained
and rinsed
2 carrots, peeled and diced
salt and freshly ground
black pepper
225 g/8 oz fresh egg tagliatelle
1 tbsp freshly chopped parsley,
to garnish
crème fraîche, to serve

Heat the sunflower oil in a large frying pan. Add the sliced leek and cook, stirring frequently, for 5 minutes, or until softened. Add the pork and cook, stirring, for 4 minutes, or until sealed.

Add the crushed garlic and the paprika and cayenne peppers to the pan and stir gently until all the pork is lightly coated in the garlic and pepper mixture.

Pour in the wine and 450 ml/$^{3}/_{4}$ pint of the vegetable stock. Add the borlotti beans and carrots and season to taste with salt and pepper. Bring the sauce to the boil, then lower the heat and simmer for a further 5 minutes.

Meanwhile, place the egg tagliatelle in a large saucepan of lightly salted, boiling water, cover and simmer for 5 minutes, or until the pasta is cooked *al dente*.

Drain the pasta, then add to the pork ragù; toss well. Adjust the seasoning, then tip into a warmed serving dish. Sprinkle with chopped parsley and serve with a little crème fraîche.

Sausage Redcurrant Pasta Bake

Serves 4

450 g/1 lb good quality, thick
pork sausages
2 tsp sunflower oil
25 g/1 oz butter
1 onion, peeled and sliced
2 tbsp plain white flour
450 ml/³/₄ pint chicken stock
150 ml/¹/₄ pint port or good
quality red wine
1 tbsp freshly chopped thyme
leaves, plus sprigs to garnish
1 bay leaf
4 tbsp redcurrant jelly
salt and freshly ground
black pepper
350 g/12 oz fresh penne
75 g/3 oz Gruyère cheese, grated

Preheat the oven to 220°C/425°F/Gas Mark 7, 15 minutes before cooking. Prick the sausages, place in a shallow ovenproof dish and toss in the sunflower oil. Cook in the oven for 25–30 minutes, or until golden brown.

Meanwhile, melt the butter in a frying pan, add the sliced onion and fry for 5 minutes, or until golden-brown. Stir in the flour and cook for 2 minutes. Remove the pan from the heat and gradually stir in the chicken stock with the port or red wine.

Return the pan to the heat and bring to the boil, stirring continuously until the sauce starts to thicken. Add the thyme, bay leaf and redcurrant jelly and season well with salt and pepper. Simmer the sauce for 5 minutes.

Bring a large pan of salted water to a rolling boil, add the pasta and cook for about 4 minutes, or until *al dente*. Drain thoroughly and reserve.

Lower the oven temperature to 200°C/400°F/Gas Mark 6. Remove the sausages from the oven, drain off any excess fat and return the sausages to the dish. Add the pasta. Pour over the sauce, removing the bay leaf, and toss together. Sprinkle with the Gruyère cheese and return to the oven for 15–20 minutes, or until bubbling and golden-brown. Serve immediately, garnished with thyme sprigs.

Pappardelle Pork with Brandy Sauce

Serves 4

4 pork fillets, each weighing
about 175 g/6 oz
1 tbsp freshly chopped sage, plus
whole leaves to garnish
salt and freshly ground
black pepper
4 slices Parma ham
1 tbsp olive oil
6 tbsp brandy
300 ml/ $1/2$ pint chicken stock
200 ml/7 fl oz double cream
350 g/12 oz pappardelle
1–2 tsp butter
2 tbsp freshly chopped
flat-leaf parsley

Preheat the oven to 200°C/400°F/Gas Mark 6, 15 minutes before cooking. Using a sharp knife, cut two slits in each pork fillet then stuff each slit with chopped sage. Season well with salt and pepper and wrap each fillet with a slice of Parma ham.

Heat the oil in a large frying pan. Add the wrapped pork fillets and cook, turning once, for 1–2 minutes, or until the ham is golden brown. Transfer to a roasting tin and cook in the preheated oven for 10–12 minutes.

Return the frying pan to the heat and add the brandy, scraping the bottom of the pan with a spoon to release all the flavours. Boil for 1 minute, then pour in the chicken stock. Boil for a further 2 minutes then pour in the cream and boil again for 2–3 minutes, or until the sauce has thickened slightly. Season the brandy sauce to taste.

Bring a large pan of lightly salted water to a rolling boil. Add the pasta and cook according to the packet instructions, or until *al dente*. Drain the pasta thoroughly and return to the pan. Add the butter and chopped parsley and toss together. Keep the pasta warm.

Remove the pork from the oven and pour any juices into the brandy sauce. Pile the pasta on individual plates, season with pepper, spoon over the brandy sauce and serve immediately with the pork fillets.

Tagliatelle with Spicy Sausage Ragù

Serves 4

3 tbsp olive oil
6 spicy sausages
1 small onion, peeled and
finely chopped
1 tsp fennel seeds
175 g/6 oz fresh pork mince
225 g can chopped tomatoes
with garlic
1 tbsp sun-dried tomato paste
2 tbsp red wine or port
salt and freshly ground
black pepper
350 g/12 oz tagliatelle
300 ml/ ½ pint prepared white
sauce (see page 116)
50 g/2 oz freshly grated
Parmesan cheese

Preheat the oven to 200°C/400°F/Gas Mark 6, 15 minutes before cooking. Heat 1 tablespoon of the olive oil in a large frying pan. Prick the sausages, add to the pan and cook for 8–10 minutes, or until browned and cooked through. Remove and cut into thin diagonal slices. Reserve.

Return the pan to the heat and pour in the remaining olive oil. Add the onion and cook for 8 minutes, or until softened. Add the fennel seeds and minced pork and cook, stirring, for 5–8 minutes, or until the meat is sealed and browned.

Stir in the tomatoes, tomato paste and the wine or port. Season to taste with salt and pepper. Bring to the boil, cover and simmer for 30 minutes, stirring occasionally. Remove the lid and simmer for 10 minutes.

Bring a large pan of lightly salted water to a rolling boil. Add the pasta and cook according to the packet instructions, or until *al dente*. Drain thoroughly and toss with the meat sauce.

Place half the pasta in an ovenproof dish, and cover with 4 tablespoons of the white sauce. Top with half the sausages and grated Parmesan cheese. Repeat the layering, finishing with white sauce and Parmesan cheese. Bake in the preheated oven for 20 minutes, until golden-brown. Serve immediately.

Gnocchi ✽ Parma Ham Bake

Serves 4

3 tbsp olive oil
1 red onion, peeled and sliced
2 garlic cloves, peeled
175 g/6 oz plum tomatoes,
skinned and quartered
2 tbsp sun-dried tomato paste
250 g tub mascarpone cheese
salt and freshly ground
black pepper
1 tbsp freshly chopped tarragon
300 g/11 oz fresh gnocchi
125 g/4 oz Cheddar or Parmesan
cheese, grated
50 g/2 oz fresh white breadcrumbs
50 g/2 oz Parma ham, sliced
10 pitted green olives, halved
sprigs of flat leaf parsley,
to garnish

Heat the oven to 180°C/350°F/Gas Mark 4, 10 minutes before cooking. Heat 2 tablespoons of the olive oil in a large frying pan and cook the onion and garlic for 5 minutes, or until softened. Stir in the tomatoes, sun-dried tomato paste and mascarpone cheese. Season to taste with salt and pepper. Add half the tarragon. Bring to the boil, then lower the heat immediately and simmer for 5 minutes.

Meanwhile, bring 1.7 litres/3 pints water to the boil in a large pan. Add the remaining olive oil and a good pinch of salt. Add the gnocchi and cook for 1–2 minutes, or until they rise to the surface.

Drain the gnocchi thoroughly and transfer to a large ovenproof dish. Add the tomato sauce and toss gently to coat the pasta. Combine the Cheddar or Parmesan cheese with the breadcrumbs and remaining tarragon and scatter over the pasta mixture. Top with the Parma ham and olives and season again.

Cook in the preheated oven for 20–25 minutes, or until golden and bubbling. Serve immediately, garnished with parsley sprigs.

Lamb Arrabbiata

Serves 4

4 tbsp olive oil
450 g/1 lb lamb fillets, cubed
1 large onion, peeled and sliced
4 garlic cloves, peeled and
finely chopped
1 red chilli, deseeded and
finely chopped
400 g can chopped tomatoes
175 g/6 oz pitted black
olives, halved
150 ml/ ¼ pint white wine
salt and freshly ground
black pepper
275 g/10 oz farfalle pasta
1 tsp butter
4 tbsp freshly chopped parsley, plus
1 tbsp to garnish

Heat 2 tablespoons of the olive oil in a large frying pan and cook the lamb for 5–7 minutes, or until sealed. Remove from the pan using a slotted spoon and reserve.

Heat the remaining oil in the pan, add the onion, garlic and chilli and cook until softened. Add the tomatoes, bring to the boil, then simmer for 10 minutes.

Return the browned lamb to the pan with the olives and pour in the wine. Bring the sauce back to the boil, reduce the heat then simmer, uncovered, for 15 minutes, until the lamb is tender. Season to taste with salt and pepper.

Meanwhile, bring a large pan of lightly salted water to a rolling boil. Add the pasta and cook according to the packet instructions, or until *al dente*.

Drain the pasta, toss in the butter, then add to the sauce and mix lightly. Stir in 4 tablespoons of the chopped parsley, then tip into a warmed serving dish. Sprinkle with the remaining parsley and serve immediately.

Creamed Lamb & Wild Mushroom Pasta

Serves 4

25 g/1 oz dried porcini
450 g/1 lb pasta shapes
25g/1 oz butter
1 tbsp olive oil
350 g/12 oz lamb neck fillet,
thinly sliced
1 garlic clove, peeled and crushed
225 g/8 oz brown or wild
mushrooms, wiped and sliced
4 tbsp white wine
125 ml/4 fl oz double cream
salt and freshly ground
black pepper
1 tbsp freshly chopped parsley,
to garnish
freshly grated Parmesan cheese,
to serve

Place the porcini in a small bowl and cover with almost boiling water. Leave to soak for 30 minutes. Drain the porcini, reserving the soaking liquid. Chop the porcini finely.

Bring a large pan of lightly salted water to a rolling boil. Add the pasta and cook according to the packet instructions, or until *al dente*.

Meanwhile, melt the butter with the olive oil in a large frying pan and fry the lamb to seal. Add the garlic, mushrooms and prepared porcini and cook for 5 minutes, or until just soft.

Add the wine and the reserved porcini soaking liquid, then simmer for 2 minutes. Stir in the cream with the seasoning and simmer for 1–2 minutes, or until just thickened.

Drain the pasta thoroughly, reserving about 4 tablespoons of the cooking water. Return the pasta to the pan. Pour over the mushroom sauce and toss lightly together, adding the pasta water if the sauce is too thick. Tip into a warmed serving dish or spoon on to individual plates. Garnish with the chopped parsley and serve immediately with grated Parmesan cheese.

Gammon with Red Wine Sauce & Pasta

Serves 2

25 g/1 oz butter
150 ml/ $^1/_4$ pint red wine
4 red onions, peeled and sliced
4 tbsp orange juice
1 tsp soft brown sugar
225 g/8 oz gammon steak, trimmed
freshly ground black pepper
175 g/6 oz fusilli
3 tbsp wholegrain mustard
2 tbsp freshly chopped flat-leaf
parsley, plus sprigs to garnish

Preheat the grill to a medium heat before cooking. Heat the butter with the red wine in a large heavy-based pan. Add the onions, cover with a tight fitting lid and cook over a very low heat for 30 minutes, or until softened and transparent. Remove the lid from the pan, stir in the orange juice and sugar, then increase the heat and cook for about 10 minutes, until the onions are golden.

Meanwhile cook the gammon steak under the preheated grill, turning at least once, for 4–6 minutes, or until tender. Cut the cooked gammon into bite-sized pieces. Reserve and keep warm.

Meanwhile, bring a large pan of very lightly salted water to a rolling boil. Add the pasta and cook according to the packet instructions, or until *al dente*. Drain the pasta thoroughly, return to the pan, season with a little pepper and keep warm.

Stir the wholegrain mustard and chopped parsley into the onion sauce then pour over the pasta. Add the gammon pieces to the pan and toss lightly to thoroughly coat the pasta with the sauce. Pile the pasta mixture on to two warmed serving plates. Garnish with sprigs of flat-leaf parsley and serve immediately.

Prosciutto Gruyère Carbonara

Serves 4

3 medium egg yolks
50 g/2 oz Gruyère cheese, grated
2 tbsp olive oil
2 garlic cloves, peeled and crushed
2 shallots, peeled and
finely chopped
200 g/7 oz prosciutto ham, cut
into strips
4 tbsp dry vermouth
salt and freshly ground
black pepper
450 g/1 lb spaghetti
15 g/ ¹/₂ oz butter
1 tbsp freshly shredded basil leaves
basil sprigs, to garnish

Place the egg yolks with 6 tablespoons of the Gruyère cheese in a bowl and mix lightly until well blended, then reserve.

Heat the olive oil in a large pan and cook the garlic and shallots for 5 minutes, or until golden-brown. Add the prosciutto ham, then cook for a further 1 minute. Pour in the dry vermouth and simmer for 2 minutes, then remove from the heat. Season to taste with salt and pepper and keep warm.

Meanwhile, bring a large pan of lightly salted water to a rolling boil. Add the pasta and cook according to the packet instructions, or until *al dente*. Drain thoroughly, reserving 4 tablespoons of the water, and return the pasta to the pan.

Remove from the heat, then add the egg and cheese mixture with the butter to the pasta; toss lightly until coated. Add the prosciutto mixture and toss again, adding the reserved pasta water, if needed, to moisten. Season to taste and sprinkle with the remaining Gruyère cheese and the shredded basil leaves. Garnish with basil sprigs and serve immediately.

Gnocchi with Tuscan Beef Ragù

Serves 4

25 g/1 oz dried porcini
3 tbsp olive oil
1 small onion, peeled and
finely chopped
1 carrot, peeled and finely chopped
1 celery, trimmed and finely chopped
1 fennel bulb, trimmed and sliced
2 garlic cloves, peeled and crushed
450 g/1 lb fresh beef steak mince
4 tbsp red wine
50 g/2 oz pine nuts
1 tbsp freshly chopped rosemary
2 tbsp tomato paste
400 g can chopped tomatoes
225 g/8 oz fresh gnocchi
salt and freshly ground
black pepper
100 g/4 oz mozzarella cheese, cubed

Preheat the oven to 200°C/400°F/Gas Mark 6, 15 minutes before cooking. Place the porcini in a small bowl and cover with almost boiling water. Leave to soak for 30 minutes. Drain, reserving the soaking liquid and straining it through a muslin-lined sieve. Chop the porcini.

Heat the olive oil in a large heavy-based pan. Add the onion, carrot, celery, fennel and garlic and cook for 8 minutes, stirring, or until soft. Add the minced steak and cook, stirring, for 5–8 minutes, or until sealed and any lumps are broken up.

Pour in the wine, then add the porcini with half the pine nuts, the rosemary and tomato paste. Stir in the porcini soaking liquid then simmer for 5 minutes. Add the chopped tomatoes and simmer gently for about 40 minutes, stirring occasionally.

Meanwhile, bring 1.7 litres/3 pints of lightly salted water to a rolling boil in a large pan. Add the gnocchi and cook for 1–2 minutes, until they rise to the surface.

Drain the gnocchi and place in an ovenproof dish. Stir in three-quarters of the mozzarella cheese with the beef sauce. Top with the remaining mozzarella and pine nuts, then bake in the preheated oven for 20 minutes, until golden-brown. Serve immediately.

Poultry

From filled pasta to baked dishes, this chapter showcases the tastiest poultry and game pasta dishes around. Whether you prefer chicken, duck or turkey, there is something to suit every taste. For an everyday lunch with a twist, the Hot Duck Pasta Salad is not to be missed, whilst the Herb-baked Chicken with Tagliatelle is the perfect warming family meal.

Hot Duck Pasta Salad

Serves 6

3 boneless and skinless
duck breasts
1 tbsp wholegrain mustard
1 tbsp clear honey
salt and freshly ground
black pepper
4 medium eggs
450 g/1 lb fusilli
125 g/4 oz French beans, trimmed
1 large carrot, peeled and cut into
thin batons
125 g/4 oz sweetcorn kernels,
cooked if frozen
75 g/3 oz fresh baby spinach
leaves, shredded

For the dressing:

8 tbsp French dressing
1 tsp horseradish sauce
4 tbsp crème fraîche

Preheat the oven to 200°C/400°F/Gas Mark 6. Place the duck breasts on a baking tray lined with tinfoil. Mix together the wholegrain mustard and honey, season lightly with salt and pepper then spread over the duck breasts. Roast in the preheated oven for 20–30 minutes, or until tender. Remove from the oven and keep warm.

Meanwhile, place the eggs in a small saucepan, cover with water and bring to the boil. Simmer for 8 minutes, then drain. As soon as the eggs are cooked, remove them from the pan and place in a bowl of very cold water to prevent dark rings forming around the yolk.

Bring a large pan of lightly salted water to a rolling boil. Add the beans and pasta, return to the boil and cook according to the packet instructions, or until *al dente*. Drain the pasta and beans and refresh under cold running water.

Place the pasta and beans in a bowl, add the carrot, sweetcorn and spinach leaves and toss lightly. Shell the eggs, cut into wedges and arrange on top of the pasta. Slice the duck breasts then place them on top of the salad. Beat the dressing ingredients together in a bowl until well blended, then drizzle over the salad. Serve immediately.

Chicken Tagliatelle

Serves 4

350 g/12 oz tagliatelle
125 g/4 oz frozen peas
4 boneless and skinless
chicken breasts
2 tbsp olive oil
$^1/_4$ cucumber, cut into strips
150 ml/$^1/_4$ pint dry vermouth
150 ml/$^1/_4$ pint double cream
125 g/4 oz Stilton cheese, crumbled
3 tbsp freshly snipped chives, plus
extra to garnish
salt and freshly ground
black pepper
fresh herbs, to garnish

Bring a large pan of lightly salted water to a rolling boil. Add the pasta and cook according to the packet instructions, or until *al dente*. Add the peas to the pan 5 minutes before the end of cooking time and cook until tender. Drain the pasta and peas, return to the pan and keep warm.

Trim the chicken if necessary, then cut into bite-sized pieces. Heat the olive oil in a large frying pan, add the chicken and cook for 8 minutes, or until golden, stirring occasionally.

Add the cucumber and cook for 2 minutes, or until slightly softened, stirring occasionally. Stir in the vermouth, bring to the boil, then lower the heat and simmer for 3 minutes, or until reduced slightly.

Add the cream to the pan, bring to the boil, stirring constantly, then stir in the Stilton cheese and snipped chives. Season to taste with salt and pepper. Heat through thoroughly, stirring occasionally, until the cheese is just beginning to melt.

Toss the chicken mixture into the pasta. Tip into a warmed serving dish or on to individual plates. Garnish and serve immediately.

Mixed Vegetable Chicken Pasta

Serves 4

3 boneless and skinless
chicken breasts
2 leeks
1 red onion
350 g/12 oz pasta shells
25 g/1 oz butter
2 tbsp olive oil
1 garlic clove, peeled and chopped
175 g/6 oz cherry tomatoes, halved
200 ml/7 fl oz double cream
425 g can asparagus tips, drained
salt and freshly ground
black pepper
125 g/4 oz double Gloucester
cheese with chives, crumbled
green salad, to serve

Preheat the grill just before using. Cut the chicken into thin strips. Trim the leeks, leaving some of the dark green tops, then shred and wash thoroughly in cold water. Peel the onion and cut into thin wedges.

Bring a large pan of lightly salted water to a rolling boil. Add the pasta and cook according to the packet instructions, or until *al dente*.

Meanwhile, melt butter with the olive oil in a large heavy-based pan, add the chicken and cook, stirring occasionally, for 8 minutes, or until browned all over. Add the leeks and onion and cook for 5 minutes, or until softened. Add the garlic and cherry tomatoes and cook for a further 2 minutes.

Stir the cream and asparagus tips into the chicken and vegetable mixture, bring to the boil slowly, then remove from the heat. Drain the pasta thoroughly and return to the pan. Pour the sauce over the pasta, season to taste with salt and pepper, then toss lightly.

Tip the pasta mixture into a gratin dish and sprinkle with the cheese. Cook under the preheated grill for 5 minutes, or until bubbling and golden, turning the dish occasionally. Serve immediately with a fresh green salad.

Herb-baked Chicken with Tagliatelle

Serves 4

75 g/3 oz fresh white breadcrumbs
3 tbsp olive oil
1 tsp dried oregano
2 tbsp sun-dried tomato paste
salt and freshly ground
black pepper
4 boneless and skinless chicken
breasts, each about 150 g/5 oz
2 x 400 g cans plum tomatoes
4 tbsp freshly chopped basil
2 tbsp dry white wine
350 g/12 oz tagliatelle
fresh basil sprigs, to garnish

Preheat the oven to 200°C/400°F/Gas Mark 6, 15 minutes before cooking. Mix together the breadcrumbs, 1 tablespoon of the olive oil, the oregano and tomato paste. Season to taste with salt and pepper. Place the chicken breasts well apart in a roasting tin and coat with the breadcrumb mixture.

Mix the plum tomatoes with the chopped basil and white wine. Season to taste, then spoon evenly round the chicken.

Drizzle the remaining olive oil over the chicken breasts and cook in the preheated oven for 20–30 minutes, or until the chicken is golden and the juices run clear when a skewer is inserted into the flesh.

Meanwhile, bring a large pan of lightly salted water to a rolling boil. Add the pasta and cook according to the packet instructions, or until *al dente*.

Drain the pasta thoroughly and transfer to warmed serving plates. Arrange the chicken breasts on top of the pasta and spoon over the sauce. Garnish with sprigs of basil and serve immediately.

Creamy Turkey Tomato Pasta

Serves 4

4 tbsp olive oil
450 g/1 lb turkey breasts, cut into
bite-sized pieces
550 g/1¼ lb cherry tomatoes,
on the vine
2 garlic cloves, peeled
and chopped
4 tbsp balsamic vinegar
4 tbsp freshly chopped basil
salt and freshly ground
black pepper
200 ml tub crème fraîche
350 g/12 oz tagliatelle
shaved Parmesan cheese,
to garnish

Preheat the oven to 200°C/400°F/Gas Mark 6. Heat 2 tablespoons of the olive oil in a large frying pan. Add the turkey and cook for 5 minutes, or until sealed, turning occasionally. Transfer to a roasting tin and add the remaining olive oil, the vine tomatoes, garlic and balsamic vinegar. Stir well and season to taste with salt and pepper. Cook in the preheated oven for 30 minutes, or until the turkey is tender, turning the tomatoes and turkey once.

Meanwhile, bring a large pan of lightly salted water to a rolling boil. Add the pasta and cook according to the packet instructions, or until *al dente*. Drain, return to the pan and keep warm. Stir the basil and seasoning into the crème fraîche.

Remove the roasting tin from the oven and discard the vines. Stir the crème fraîche and basil mix into the turkey and tomato mixture and return to the oven for 1–2 minutes, or until thoroughly heated through.

Stir the turkey and tomato mixture into the pasta and toss lightly together. Tip into a warmed serving dish. Garnish with Parmesan cheese shavings and serve immediately.

Parma Ham-wrapped Chicken with Ribbon Pasta

Serves 4

4 boneless and skinless
chicken breasts
salt and freshly ground
black pepper
12 slices Parma ham
2 tbsp olive oil
350 g/12 oz ribbon pasta
1 garlic clove, peeled and chopped
1 bunch spring onions, trimmed
and diagonally sliced
400 g can chopped tomatoes
juice of 1 lemon
150 ml/¼ pint crème fraîche
3 tbsp freshly chopped parsley
pinch of sugar
freshly grated Parmesan cheese,
to garnish

Cut each chicken breast into 3 pieces and season well with salt and pepper. Wrap each chicken piece in a slice of Parma ham to enclose completely, securing if necessary with either fine twine or cocktail sticks.

Heat the oil in a large frying pan and cook the Parma Ham-wrapped chicken, turning occasionally, for 12–15 minutes, or until thoroughly cooked. Remove from the pan with a slotted spoon and reserve.

Meanwhile, bring a large pan of lightly salted water to a rolling boil. Add the pasta and cook according to the packet instructions, or until *al dente*.

Add the garlic and spring onions to the frying pan and cook, stirring occasionally, for 2 minutes, or until softened. Stir in the tomatoes, lemon juice and crème fraîche. Bring to the boil, lower the heat and simmer, covered, for 3 minutes. Stir in the parsley and sugar, season to taste, then return the chicken to the pan and heat for 2–3 minutes, or until piping hot.

Drain the pasta thoroughly and mix in the chopped parsley, then spoon on to a warmed serving dish or individual plates. Arrange the chicken and sauce over the pasta. Garnish and serve immediately.

Baked Aubergines with Tomato & Mozzarella

Serves 4

3 medium aubergines, trimmed and sliced
salt and freshly ground black pepper
4–6 tbsp olive oil
450 g/1 lb fresh turkey mince
1 onion, peeled and chopped
2 garlic cloves, peeled and chopped
2 x 400 g cans cherry tomatoes
1 tbsp fresh mixed herbs
200 ml/7 fl oz red wine
350 g/12 oz macaroni
5 tbsp freshly chopped basil
125 g/4 oz mozzarella cheese, drained and chopped
50 g/2 oz freshly grated Parmesan cheese

Preheat the oven to 200°C/400°F/Gas Mark 6, 15 minutes before cooking. Place the aubergine slices in a colander and sprinkle with salt. Leave for 1 hour or until the juices run clear. Rinse and dry on absorbent kitchen paper. Heat 3–5 tablespoons of the olive oil in a large frying pan and cook the prepared aubergines in batches for 2 minutes on each side, or until softened. Remove and drain on absorbent kitchen paper.

Heat 1 tablespoon of olive oil in a saucepan, add the turkey mince and cook for 5 minutes, or until browned and sealed. Add the onion to the pan and cook for 5 minutes, or until softened. Add the chopped garlic, the tomatoes and mixed herbs. Pour in the wine and season to taste with salt and pepper. Bring to the boil, lower the heat then simmer for 15 minutes, or until thickened.

Meanwhile, bring a large pan of lightly salted water to a rolling boil. Add the macaroni and cook according to the packet instructions, or until *al dente*. Drain thoroughly.

Spoon half the tomato mixture into a lightly oiled ovenproof dish. Top with half the aubergine, pasta and chopped basil, then season lightly. Repeat the layers, finishing with a layer of aubergine. Sprinkle with the mozzarella and Parmesan cheeses, then bake in the preheated oven for 30 minutes, or until golden and bubbling. Serve immediately.

Mini Chicken Balls with Tagliatelle

Serves 4

450 g/1 lb fresh chicken mince
50 g/2 oz sun-dried tomatoes,
drained and finely chopped
salt and freshly ground
black pepper
25 g/1 oz butter
1 tbsp oil
350 g/12 oz leeks, trimmed and
diagonally sliced
125 g/4 oz frozen broad beans
300 ml/ ½ pint single cream
50 g/2 oz freshly grated
Parmesan cheese
350 g/12 oz tagliatelle
4 medium eggs
fresh herbs, to garnish

Mix the chicken and tomatoes together and season to taste with salt and pepper. Divide the mixture into 32 pieces and roll into balls. Transfer to a baking sheet, cover and leave in the refrigerator for 1 hour.

Melt the butter in a large frying pan, add the chicken balls and cook for 5 minutes, or until golden, turning occasionally. Remove, drain on absorbent kitchen paper and keep warm.

Add the leeks and broad beans to the frying pan and cook, stirring, for 10 minutes or until cooked and tender. Return the chicken balls to the pan, then stir in the cream and Parmesan cheese and heat through.

Meanwhile, bring a large pan of lightly salted water to a rolling boil. Add the pasta and cook according to the packet instructions, or until *al dente*.

Bring a separate frying pan full of water to the boil, crack in the eggs and simmer for 2–4 minutes, or until poached to personal preference.

Meanwhile, drain the pasta thoroughly and return to the pan. Pour the chicken ball and vegetable sauce over the pasta, toss lightly and heat through for 1–2 minutes. Arrange on warmed individual plates and top with the poached eggs. Garnish with fresh herbs and serve immediately.

Pasta Pepper Salad

Serves 4

4 tbsp olive oil
1 red, orange and yellow pepper,
deseeded and cut into chunks
1 large courgette, trimmed and cut
into chunks
1 medium aubergine, trimmed
and diced
275 g/10 oz fusilli
4 plum tomatoes, quartered
1 bunch fresh basil leaves,
roughly chopped
2 tbsp pesto
2 garlic cloves, peeled and
roughly chopped
1 tbsp lemon juice
225 g/8 oz boneless and skinless
roasted chicken breast
salt and freshly ground
black pepper
125 g/4 oz feta cheese, crumbled
crusty bread, to serve

Preheat the oven to 200°C/400°F/Gas Mark 6. Spoon the olive oil into a roasting tin and heat in the oven for 2 minutes, or until almost smoking. Remove from the oven, add the peppers, courgette and aubergine and stir until coated. Bake for 30 minutes, or until charred, stirring occasionally.

Bring a large pan of lightly salted water to a rolling boil. Add the pasta and cook according to the packet instructions, or until *al dente*. Drain and refresh under cold running water. Drain thoroughly, place in a large salad bowl and reserve.

Remove the cooked vegetables from the oven and allow to cool. Add to the cooled pasta, together with the quartered tomatoes, chopped basil leaves, pesto, garlic and lemon juice. Toss lightly to mix.

Shred the chicken roughly into small pieces and stir into the pasta and vegetable mixture. Season to taste with salt and pepper, then sprinkle the crumbled feta cheese over the pasta and stir gently. Cover the dish and leave to marinate for 30 minutes, stirring occasionally. Serve the salad with fresh crusty bread.

Turkey & Oven-roasted Vegetable Salad

Serves 4

6 tbsp olive oil
3 medium courgettes, trimmed and sliced
2 yellow peppers, deseeded and sliced
125 g/4 oz pine nuts
275 g/10 oz macaroni
350 g/12 oz cooked turkey
280 g jar or can chargrilled artichokes, drained and sliced
225 g/8 oz baby plum tomatoes, quartered
4 tbsp freshly chopped coriander
1 garlic clove, peeled and chopped
3 tbsp balsamic vinegar
salt and freshly ground black pepper

Preheat the oven to 200°C/400°F/Gas Mark 6, 15 minutes before cooking. Line a large roasting tin with tinfoil, pour in half the olive oil and place in the oven for 3 minutes, or until very hot. Remove from the oven, add the courgettes and peppers and stir until evenly coated in the oil. Bake for 30–35 minutes, or until slightly charred, turning occasionally.

Add the pine nuts to the tin. Return to the oven and bake for 10 minutes, or until the pine nuts are toasted. Remove from the oven and allow the vegetables to cool completely.

Bring a large pan of lightly salted water to a rolling boil. Add the macaroni and cook according to the packet instructions, or until *al dente*. Drain and refresh under cold running water then drain thoroughly and place in a large salad bowl.

Cut the turkey into bite-sized pieces and add to the macaroni. Add the artichokes and tomatoes with the cooled vegetables and pan juices to the pan. Blend together the coriander, garlic, remaining oil, vinegar and seasoning. Pour over the salad, toss lightly and serve.

Spicy Chicken Pasta Salad

Serves 6

450 g/1 lb pasta shells
25 g/1 oz butter
1 onion, peeled and chopped
2 tbsp mild curry paste
125 g/4 oz ready-to-eat dried
apricots, chopped
2 tbsp tomato paste
3 tbsp mango chutney
300 ml/ ¹/₂ pint mayonnaise
425 g can pineapple slices in
fruit juice
salt and freshly ground
black pepper
450 g/1 lb skinned and boned
cooked chicken, cut into
bite-sized pieces
25 g/1 oz flaked toasted
almond slivers
coriander sprigs, to garnish

Bring a large pan of lightly salted water to a rolling boil. Add the pasta shells and cook according to the packet instructions, or until *al dente*. Drain and refresh under cold running water then drain thoroughly and place in a large serving bowl.

Meanwhile, melt the butter in a heavy-based pan, add the onion and cook for 5 minutes, or until softened. Add the curry paste and cook, stirring, for 2 minutes. Stir in the apricots and tomato paste, then cook for 1 minute. Remove from the heat and allow to cool.

Blend the mango chutney and mayonnaise together in a small bowl. Drain the pineapple slices, adding 2 tablespoons of the pineapple juice to the mayonnaise mixture; reserve the pineapple slices. Season the mayonnaise to taste with salt and pepper.

Cut the pineapple slices into chunks and stir into the pasta together with the mayonnaise mixture, curry paste and cooked chicken pieces. Toss lightly together to coat the pasta. Sprinkle with the almond slivers, garnish with coriander sprigs and serve.

Chicken Gorgonzola Mushroom Macaroni

Serves 4

450 g/1 lb macaroni
75 g/3 oz butter
225 g/8 oz chestnut mushrooms,
wiped and sliced
225 g/8 oz baby button mushrooms,
wiped and halved
350 g/12 oz cooked chicken,
skinned and chopped
2 tsp cornflour
300 ml/ ½ pint semi-skimmed milk
50 g/2 oz Gorgonzola cheese,
chopped, plus extra to serve
2 tbsp freshly chopped sage
1 tbsp freshly chopped chives, plus
extra chive leaves to garnish
salt and freshly ground
black pepper

Bring a large pan of lightly salted water to a rolling boil. Add the macaroni and cook according to the packet instructions, or until *al dente*.

Meanwhile, melt the butter in a large frying pan, add the chestnut and button mushrooms and cook for 5 minutes, or until golden, stirring occasionally. Add the chicken to the pan and cook for 4 minutes, or until heated through thoroughly and slightly golden, stirring occasionally.

Blend the cornflour with a little of the milk in a jug to form a smooth paste, then gradually blend in the remaining milk and pour into the frying pan. Bring to the boil slowly, stirring constantly. Add cheese and cook for 1 minute, stirring frequently until melted.

Stir the sage and chives into the frying pan. Season to taste with salt and pepper then heat through. Drain the macaroni thoroughly and return to the pan. Pour the chicken and mushroom sauce over the macaroni and toss lightly to coat. Tip into a warmed serving dish, and serve immediately with extra Gorgonzola cheese.

Spaghetti with Turkey Bacon Sauce

Serves 4

450 g/1 lb spaghetti
25 g /1 oz butter
225 g/8 oz smoked streaky bacon,
rind removed
350 g/12 oz fresh turkey strips
1 onion, peeled and chopped
1 garlic clove, peeled and chopped
3 medium eggs, beaten
300 ml/ ½ pint double cream
salt and freshly ground
black pepper
50 g/2 oz freshly grated
Parmesan cheese
2–3 tbsp freshly chopped
coriander, to garnish

Bring a large pan of lightly salted water to a rolling boil. Add the spaghetti and cook according to the packet instructions, or until *al dente*.

Meanwhile, melt the butter in a large frying pan. Using a sharp knife, cut the streaky bacon into small dice. Add the bacon to the pan with the turkey strips and cook for 8 minutes, or until browned, stirring occasionally to prevent sticking. Add the onion and garlic and cook for 5 minutes, or until softened, stirring occasionally.

Place the eggs and cream in a bowl and season to taste with salt and pepper. Beat together then pour into the frying pan and cook, stirring, for 2 minutes or until the mixture begins to thicken but does not scramble.

Drain the spaghetti thoroughly and return to the pan. Pour over the sauce, add the grated Parmesan cheese and toss lightly. Heat through for 2 minutes, or until piping hot. Tip into a warmed serving dish and sprinkle with freshly chopped coriander. Serve immediately.

Cheesy Baked Chicken Macaroni

Serves 4

1 tbsp olive oil
350 g/12 oz boneless and skinless
chicken breasts, diced
75 g/3 oz pancetta, diced
1 onion, peeled and chopped
1 garlic clove, peeled and chopped
350 g packet fresh tomato sauce
400 g can chopped tomatoes
2 tbsp freshly chopped basil, plus
leaves to garnish
salt and freshly ground
black pepper
350 g/12 oz macaroni
150 g/5 oz mozzarella cheese,
drained and chopped
50 g/2 oz Gruyère cheese, grated
50 g/2 oz freshly grated
Parmesan cheese

Preheat the grill just before cooking. Heat the oil in large frying pan and cook the chicken for 8 minutes, or until browned, stirring occasionally. Drain on absorbent kitchen paper and reserve. Add the pancetta slices to the pan and fry on both sides until crispy. Remove from the pan and reserve.

Add the onion and garlic to the frying pan and cook for 5 minutes, or until softened. Stir in the tomato sauce, chopped tomatoes and basil and season to taste with salt and pepper. Bring to the boil, lower the heat and simmer the sauce for 5 minutes.

Meanwhile, bring a large pan of lightly salted water to a rolling boil. Add the macaroni and cook according to the packet instructions, or until *al dente*.

Drain the macaroni thoroughly, return to the pan and stir in the sauce, chicken and mozzarella cheese. Spoon into a shallow ovenproof dish.

Sprinkle the pancetta over the macaroni. Sprinkle over the Gruyère and Parmesan cheeses. Place under the preheated grill and cook for 5–10 minutes, or until golden-brown; turn the dish occasionally. Garnish and serve immediately.

Pesto Chicken Tagliatelle

Serves 4

2 tbsp olive oil
350 g/12 oz boneless and skinless
chicken breasts, cut into chunks
75 g/3 oz butter
2 medium leeks, trimmed and
sliced thinly
125 g/4 oz oyster mushrooms,
trimmed and halved
200 g/7 oz small open chestnut
mushrooms, wiped and halved
450 g/1lb fresh tagliatelle
4–6 tbsp red pesto
200 ml/7 fl oz crème fraîche
50 g/2 oz freshly grated
Parmesan cheese
salt and freshly ground black pepper

Heat the oil in a large frying pan, add the chicken and cook for
8 minutes, or until golden-brown, stirring occasionally. Using a slotted
spoon, remove the chicken from the pan, drain on absorbent kitchen
paper and reserve.

Melt the butter in the pan. Add the leeks and cook gently for
3–5 minutes, or until slightly softened, stirring occasionally. Add the
oyster and chestnut mushrooms and cook for 5 minutes, or until
browned, stirring occasionally.

Bring a large pan of lightly salted water to the boil, add the tagliatelle,
return to the boil and cook for 4 minutes, or until *al dente*.

Add the chicken, pesto and crème fraîche to the mushroom mixture.
Stir, then heat through thoroughly. Stir in the grated Parmesan cheese
and season to taste with salt and pepper.

Drain the tagliatelle thoroughly and pile on to warmed plates. Spoon
over the sauce and serve immediately.

Chicken Prawn-stacked Ravioli

Serves 4

1 tbsp olive oil
1 onion, peeled and chopped
1 garlic clove, peeled and chopped
450 g/1 lb boned and skinned
cooked chicken, cut into
large pieces
1 beefsteak tomato, deseeded
and chopped
150 ml/ ¹/₄ pint dry white wine
150 ml/ ¹/₄ pint double cream
250 g/9 oz peeled cooked prawns,
thawed if frozen
2 tbsp freshly chopped tarragon,
plus sprigs to garnish
salt and freshly ground
black pepper
8 sheets fresh lasagne

Heat the olive oil in a large frying pan, add the onion and garlic and cook for 5 minutes, or until softened, stirring occasionally. Add the chicken pieces and fry for 4 minutes, or until heated through, turning occasionally.

Stir in the chopped tomato, wine and cream and bring to the boil. Lower the heat and simmer for about 5 minutes, or until reduced and thickened. Stir in the prawns and tarragon and season to taste with salt and pepper. Heat the sauce through gently.

Meanwhile, bring a large pan of lightly salted water to the boil and add 2 lasagne sheets. Return to the boil and cook for 2 minutes, stirring gently to avoid sticking. Remove from the pan using a slotted spoon and keep warm. Repeat with the remaining sheets.

Cut each sheet of lasagne in half. Place two pieces on each of the warmed plates and divide half of the chicken mixture among them. Top each serving with a second sheet of lasagne and divide the remainder of the chicken mixture among them. Top with a final layer of lasagne. Garnish with tarragon sprigs and serve immediately.

Penne with Pan-fried Chicken & Capers

Serves 4

4 boneless and skinless
chicken breasts
25 g/1 oz plain flour
salt and freshly ground black pepper
350 g/12 oz penne
2 tbsp olive oil
25 g/1 oz butter
1 red onion, peeled and sliced
1 garlic clove, peeled and chopped
4–6 tbsp pesto
250 g carton mascarpone cheese
1 tsp wholegrain mustard
1 tbsp lemon juice
2 tbsp freshly chopped basil
3 tbsp capers in brine, rinsed
and drained
freshly shaved Pecorino
Romano cheese

Trim the chicken and cut into bite-sized pieces. Season the flour with salt and pepper then toss the chicken in the seasoned flour and reserve.

Bring a large saucepan of lightly salted water to a rolling boil. Add the penne and cook according to the packet instructions, or until *al dente*.

Meanwhile, heat the olive oil in a large frying pan. Add the chicken to the pan and cook for 8 minutes, or until golden on all sides, stirring frequently. Transfer the chicken to a plate and reserve.

Add the onion and garlic to the oil remaining in the frying pan and cook for 5 minutes, or until softened, stirring frequently.

Return the chicken to the frying pan. Stir in the pesto and mascarpone cheese and heat through, stirring gently, until smooth. Stir in the wholegrain mustard, lemon juice, basil and capers. Season to taste, then continue to heat through until piping hot.

Drain the penne thoroughly and return to the saucepan. Pour over the sauce and toss well to coat. Arrange the pasta on individual warmed plates. Scatter with the cheese and serve immediately.

Vegetables

 Salads

Scrumptious accompanied by all manner of vegetables, pasta makes an ideal vegetarian option. Whether enjoyed hot as a main meal, or cold as a salad, these recipes will satisfy every taste craving from creamy to spicy. For a simple dinner that kids will love too, Cheesy Pasta with Tomatoes & Cream is the answer, and for vegetable lovers, look no further than Pastini Stuffed Peppers.

Spaghetti with Pesto

Serves 4

200 g/7 oz freshly grated
Parmesan cheese, plus extra
to serve
25 g/1 oz fresh basil leaves, plus
extra to garnish
6 tbsp pine nuts
3 large garlic cloves, peeled
200 ml/7 fl oz extra virgin olive oil,
plus more if necessary
salt and freshly ground pepper
400 g/14 oz spaghetti

To make the pesto, place the Parmesan cheese in a food processor with the basil leaves, pine nuts and garlic and process until well blended.

With the motor running, gradually pour in the extra virgin olive oil, until a thick sauce forms. Add a little more oil if the sauce seems too thick. Season to taste with salt and pepper. Transfer to a bowl, cover and store in the refrigerator until required.

Bring a large pan of lightly salted water to a rolling boil. Add the spaghetti and cook according to the packet instructions, or until *al dente*.

Drain the spaghetti thoroughly and return to the pan. Stir in the pesto and toss lightly. Heat through gently, then tip the pasta into a warmed serving dish or spoon on to individual plates. Garnish with basil leaves and serve immediately with extra Parmesan cheese.

Venetian Herb Orzo

Serves 4–6

200 g/7 oz baby spinach leaves
150 g/5 oz rocket leaves
50 g/2 oz flat-leaf parsley
6 spring onions, trimmed
few leaves of fresh mint
3 tbsp extra virgin olive oil, plus
more if required
450 g/11 oz orzo
salt and freshly ground
black pepper

Rinse the spinach leaves in several changes of cold water and reserve. Finely chop the rocket leaves with the parsley and mint. Thinly slice the green of the spring onions.

Bring a large saucepan of water to the boil, add the spinach leaves, herbs and spring onions and cook for about 10 seconds. Remove and rinse under cold running water. Drain well and, using your hands, squeeze out all the excess moisture.

Place the spinach, herbs and spring onions in a food processor. Blend for 1 minute then, with the motor running, gradually pour in the olive oil until the sauce is well blended.

Meanwhile, bring a large pan of lightly salted water to a rolling boil. Add the pasta and cook according to the packet instructions, or until *al dente*. Drain thoroughly and place in a large warmed bowl.

Add the spinach sauce to the orzo and stir lightly until the orzo is well coated. Stir in an extra tablespoon of olive oil if the mixture seems too thick. Season well with salt and pepper. Serve immediately on warmed plates or allow to cool to room temperature.

Cheesy Pasta with Tomatoes & Cream

Serves 4

fresh pasta dough (*see* page 14)
225 g/8 oz fresh ricotta cheese
225 g/8 oz smoked mozzarella,
grated, (use normal if smoked
is unavailable)
5 g/4 oz freshly grated pecorino or
Parmesan cheese
2 medium eggs, lightly beated
2–3 tbsp finely chopped mint,
basil or parsley
salt and freshly ground black pepper

For the sauce:

2 tbsp olive oil
1 small onion, peeled and
finely chopped
2 garlic cloves, peeled and
finely chopped
450g/1 lb ripe plum tomatoes,
peeled, deseeded and
finely chopped
50 ml/2 fl oz white vermouth
225 ml/8 fl oz double cream
fresh basil leaves, to garnish

Place the ricotta cheese in a bowl and beat until smooth, then add the remaining cheeses with the eggs, herbs and seasoning to taste. Beat well until creamy and smooth.

Cut the prepared pasta dough into quarters. Working with one quarter at a time, and covering the remaining quarters with a clean, damp tea towel, roll out the pasta very thinly. Using a 10 cm/4 inch pastry cutter or small saucer, cut out as many rounds as possible.

Place a small tablespoonful of the filling mixture slightly below the centre of each round. Lightly moisten the edge of the round with water and fold in half to form a filled half-moon shape. Using a dinner fork, press the edges together firmly. Transfer to a lightly floured baking sheet and continue filling the remaining pasta. Leave to dry for 15 minutes.

Heat the oil in a large saucepan, add the onions and cook gently for 3–4 minutes, or until beginning to soften. Add the garlic and cook for 1–2 minutes, then add the tomatoes, vermouth and cream and bring to the boil. Simmer for 10–15 minutes, or until thickened and reduced.

Bring a large saucepan of salted water to the boil. Add the pasta and return to the boil. Cook, stirring frequently, for 5 minutes, or until *al dente*. Drain, pour over the sauce, garnish with basil and serve immediately.

Pastini-stuffed Peppers

Serves 6

6 red, yellow or orange peppers,
tops cut off and deseeded
salt and freshly ground black pepper
175 g/6 oz pastini
4 tbsp olive oil
1 onion, peeled and finely chopped
2 garlic cloves, peeled and
finely chopped
3 ripe plum tomatoes, skinned,
deseeded and chopped
50 ml/2 fl oz dry white wine
8 pitted black olives, chopped
4 tbsp freshly chopped mixed herbs,
such as parsley, basil, oregano
or marjoram
125 g/4 oz mozzarella cheese, diced
4 tbsp grated Parmesan cheese
fresh tomato sauce, to serve

Preheat the oven to 190°C/375°F/Gas Mark 5, 10 minutes before cooking. Bring a pan of water to the boil. Trim the bottom of each pepper so it sits straight. Blanch the peppers for 2–3 minutes, then drain on absorbent kitchen paper.

Return the water to the boil, add ½ teaspoon of salt and the pastini and cook for 3–4 minutes, or until *al dente*. Drain thoroughly, reserving the water. Rinse under cold running water, drain again and reserve.

Heat 2 tablespoons of the olive oil in a large frying pan, add the onion and cook for 3–4 minutes. Add the garlic and cook for 1 minute. Stir in the tomatoes and wine and cook for 5 minutes, stirring frequently. Add the olives, herbs, mozzarella cheese and half the Parmesan cheese. Season to taste with salt and pepper. Remove from the heat and stir in the pastini.

Dry the insides of the peppers with absorbent kitchen paper, then season lightly. Arrange the peppers in a lightly oiled shallow baking dish and fill with the pastini mixture. Sprinkle with the remaining Parmesan cheese and drizzle over the remaining oil. Pour in boiling water to come 1 cm/½ inch up the sides of the dish. Cook in the preheated oven for 25 minutes, or until cooked. Serve immediately with freshly made tomato sauce.

Fusilli with Courgettes & Sun-dried Tomatoes

Serves 6

5 tbsp olive oil
1 large onion, peeled and thinly sliced
2 garlic cloves, peeled and finely chopped
700 g/1 1/2 lb courgettes, trimmed and sliced
400 g can chopped plum tomatoes
12 sun-dried tomatoes, cut into thin strips
salt and freshly ground black pepper
450 g/1 lb fusilli
25 g/1 oz butter, diced
2 tbsp freshly chopped basil or flat leaf parsley
grated Parmesan or pecorino cheese, for serving

Heat 2 tablespoons of the oil in a large frying pan, add the onion and cook for 5–7 minutes, or until softened. Add the chopped garlic and courgette slices and cook for a further 5 minutes, stirring occasionally.

Stir the chopped tomatoes and the sun-dried tomatoes into the frying pan and season to taste with salt and pepper. Cook until the courgettes are just tender and the sauce is slightly thickened.

Bring a large pan of lightly salted water to a rolling boil. Add the fusilli and cook according to the packet instructions, or until *al dente*.

Drain the fusilli thoroughly and return to the pan. Add the butter and remaining oil and toss to coat. Stir the chopped basil or parsley into the courgette mixture and pour over the fusilli. Toss and tip into a warmed serving dish. Serve with grated Parmesan or pecorino cheese..

Linguine with Walnut Pesto

Serves 4

125 g/4 oz walnut halves
1–2 garlic cloves, peeled and
coarsely chopped
40 g/1½ oz dried breadcrumbs
3 tbsp extra virgin olive oil
1 tbsp walnut oil
3–4 tbsp freshly chopped parsley
50 g/2 oz butter, softened
2 tbsp double cream
25 g/1 oz Parmesan cheese,
grated, plus extra to serve
salt and freshly ground
black pepper
450 g/1 lb linguine

Bring a saucepan of water to the boil. Add the walnut halves and simmer for about 1 minute. Drain and turn on to a clean tea towel. Using the towel, rub the nuts gently to loosen the skins, turn into a coarse sieve or colander and shake to separate the skins. Discard the skins and coarsely chop the nuts.

With the the food processor motor running, drop in the garlic cloves and chop finely. Remove the lid, then add the walnuts, breadcrumbs, olive and walnut oils and the parsley. Blend to a paste with a crumbly texture.

Scrape the nut mixture into a bowl, add the softened butter and, using a wooden spoon, cream them together. Gradually beat in the cream and the Parmesan cheese. Season the walnut pesto to taste with salt and pepper.

Bring a large pan of lightly salted water to a rolling boil. Add the linguine and cook according to the packet instructions, or until *al dente*.

Drain the linguine thoroughly, reserving 1–2 tablespoons of the cooking water. Return the linguine and reserved water to the pan. Add the walnut pesto, 1 tablespoon at a time, tossing and stirring until well coated. Tip into a warmed serving dish or spoon on to individual plates. Serve immediately with the extra grated Parmesan cheese.

Four-cheese Tagliatelle

Serves 4

300 ml/ ¹/₂ pint whipping cream
4 garlic cloves, peeled and
lightly bruised
75 g/3 oz fontina cheese, diced
75 g/3 oz Gruyère cheese, grated
75 g/3 oz mozzarella cheese,
preferably, diced
50 g/2 oz Parmesan cheese, grated,
plus extra to serve
salt and freshly ground
black pepper
275 g/10 oz fresh green tagliatelle
1–2 tbsp freshly snipped chives
fresh basil leaves, to garnish

Place the whipping cream with the garlic cloves in a medium pan and heat gently until small bubbles begin to form around the edge of the pan. Using a slotted spoon, remove and discard the garlic cloves.

Add all the cheeses to the pan and stir until melted. Season with a little salt and a lot of black pepper. Keep the sauce warm over a low heat, but do not allow to boil.

Meanwhile, bring a large pan of lightly salted water to the boil. Add the tagliatelle, return to the boil and cook for 2–3 minutes, or until *al dente*.

Drain the pasta thoroughly and return to the pan. Pour the sauce over the pasta, add the chives then toss lightly until well coated. Tip into a warmed serving dish or spoon on to individual plates. Garnish with a few basil leaves and serve immediately with extra Parmesan cheese.

Rigatoni with Roasted Beetroot & Rocket

Serves 4

350 g/12 oz raw baby
beetroot, unpeeled
1 garlic clove, peeled and crushed
$^{1}/_{2}$ tsp finely grated orange rind
1 tbsp orange juice
1 tsp lemon juice
2 tbsp walnut oil
salt and freshly ground
black pepper
350 g/12 oz dried fettucini
75 g/3 oz rocket leaves
125 g/4 oz Dolcelatte cheese,
cut into small cubes

Preheat oven to 150°C/300°F/Gas Mark 2, 10 minutes before cooking. Wrap the beetroot individually in tinfoil and bake for 1–1$^{1}/_{2}$ hours, or until tender. Test by opening one of the parcels and scraping the skin away from the stem end – it should come off very easily.

Leave the beetroot until cool enough to handle, then peel and cut each beetroot into 6–8 wedges, depending on the size. Mix the garlic, orange rind and juice, lemon juice, walnut oil and salt and pepper together, then drizzle over the beetroot and toss to coat well.

Meanwhile, bring a large saucepan of lightly salted water to the boil. Cook the pasta for 10 minutes, or until *al dente*.

Drain the pasta thoroughly, then add the warm beetroot, rocket leaves and Dolcelatte cheese. Quickly and gently toss together, then divide between serving bowls and serve immediately before the rocket wilts.

Tagliatelle Primavera

Serves 4

125 g/4 oz asparagus, lightly peeled
and cut into 6.5 cm/2^1/$_2$ inch lengths
125 g/4 oz carrots, peeled and cut
into julienne strips
125 g/4 oz courgettes, trimmed
and cut into julienne strips
50 g/2 oz small mangetout
50 g/2 oz butter
1 small onion, peeled and
finely chopped
1 small red pepper, deseeded
and finely chopped
50 ml/2 fl oz dry vermouth
225 ml/8 fl oz double cream
1 small leek, trimmed and cut into
julienne strips
75 g/3 oz fresh green peas
(or frozen, thawed)
salt and freshly ground black pepper
400 g/14 oz fresh tagliatelle
2 tbsp freshly chopped
flat leaf parsley
25 g/1 oz Parmesan cheese, grated

Bring a medium saucepan of salted water to a rolling boil. Add the asparagus and blanch for 1–2 minutes, or until just beginning to soften. Using a slotted spoon, transfer to a colander and rinse under cold running water. Repeat with the carrots and courgettes. Add the mangetout, return to the boil, drain, rinse immediately and drain again. Reserve the blanched vegetables.

Heat the butter in a large frying pan, add the onion and red pepper and cook gently for 5 minutes, or until they begin to soften and colour. Pour in the dry vermouth; it will bubble and steam and evaporate almost immediately. Stir in the cream and simmer over a medium-low heat until reduced by about half. Add the blanched vegetables with the leeks, peas and seasoning and heat through for 2 minutes.

Meanwhile, bring a large saucepan of lightly salted water to the boil, add the tagliatelle and return to the boil. Cook for 2–3 minutes, or until *al dente*. Drain thoroughly and return to the pan.

Stir the chopped parsley into the cream and vegetable sauce then pour over the pasta and toss to coat. Sprinkle with the grated Parmesan cheese and toss lightly. Tip into a warmed serving bowl or spoon on to individual plates and serve immediately.

Aubergine Ravioli Parmigiana

Serves 6

4 tbsp olive oil
1 large onion, peeled and
finely chopped
2–3 garlic cloves, peeled
and crushed
2 x 400 g cans chopped tomatoes
2 tsp brown sugar
1 dried bay leaf
1 tsp dried oregano
1 tsp dried basil
2 tbsp freshly shredded basil
salt and freshly ground black pepper
2–3 medium aubergines, sliced
crosswise 1 cm/^{1}/$_2$ inch thick
2 medium eggs, beaten with
1 tbsp water
125 g/4 oz dried breadcrumbs
75 g/3 oz freshly grated
Parmesan cheese
400 g/14 oz mozzarella cheese,
thinly sliced
250 g/9 oz cheese-filled ravioli,
cooked and drained

Preheat the oven to 180°C/350°F/Gas Mark 4, about 15 minutes before cooking. Heat 2 tablespoons of the olive oil in a large, heavy-based pan, add the onion and cook for 6–7 minutes, or until softened. Add the garlic, cook for 1 minute then stir in the tomatoes, sugar, bay leaf, dried oregano and basil, then bring to the boil, stirring frequently. Simmer for 30–35 minutes, or until thickened and reduced, stirring occasionally. Stir in the fresh basil and season to taste with salt and pepper. Remove the tomato sauce from the heat and reserve.

Heat the remaining olive oil in a large, heavy-based frying pan over a high heat. Dip the aubergine slices in the egg mixture then in the breadcrumbs. Cook in batches until golden on both sides. Drain on absorbent kitchen paper. Add more oil between batches if necessary.

Spoon a little tomato sauce into the base of a lightly oiled large baking dish. Cover with a layer of aubergine slices, a sprinkling of Parmesan cheese, a layer of mozzarella cheese, then more sauce. Repeat the layers then cover the sauce with a layer of cooked ravioli. Continue to layer in this way, ending with a layer of mozzarella cheese. Sprinkle the top with Parmesan cheese.

Drizzle with a little extra olive oil if liked, then bake in the preheated oven for 30 minutes, or until golden-brown and bubbling. Serve immediately.

Baked Macaroni Cheese

Serves 8

450 g/1 lb macaroni
75 g/3 oz butter
1 onion, peeled and finely chopped
40 g/1½ oz plain flour
1 litre/1¾ pints milk
1–2 dried bay leaves
½ tsp dried thyme
salt and freshly ground black pepper
cayenne pepper
freshly grated nutmeg
2 small leeks, trimmed, finely
chopped, cooked and drained
1 tbsp Dijon mustard
400 g/14 oz mature Cheddar
cheese, grated
2 tbsp dried breadcrumbs
2 tbsp freshly grated
Parmesan cheese
basil sprig, to garnish

Preheat the oven to 190°C/375°F/Gas Mark 5, 10 minutes before cooking. Bring a large pan of lightly salted water to a rolling boil. Add the macaroni and cook according to the packet instructions, or until *al dente*. Drain thoroughly and reserve.

Meanwhile, melt 50 g/2 oz of the butter in a large, heavy-based saucepan, add the onion and cook, stirring frequently, for 5–7 minutes, or until softened. Sprinkle in the flour and cook, stirring constantly, for 2 minutes. Remove the pan from the heat, stir in the milk, return to the heat and cook, stirring, until a smooth sauce has formed.

Add the bay leaf and thyme to the sauce and season to taste with salt, pepper, cayenne pepper and freshly grated nutmeg. Simmer for about 15 minutes, stirring frequently, until thickened and smooth.

Remove the sauce from the heat. Add the cooked leeks, mustard and Cheddar cheese and stir until the cheese has melted. Stir in the macaroni then tip into a lightly oiled baking dish.

Sprinkle the breadcrumbs and Parmesan cheese over the macaroni. Dot with the remaining butter, then bake in the preheated oven for 1 hour, or until golden. Garnish with a basil sprig and serve immediately.

Rigatoni with Gorgonzola & Walnuts

Serves 4

400 g/14 oz rigatoni
50 g/2 oz butter
125 g/4 oz crumbled
Gorgonzola cheese
2 tbsp brandy, optional
200 ml/7 fl oz whipping or
double cream
75 g/3 oz walnut pieces, lightly
toasted and coarsely chopped
1 tbsp freshly chopped basil
50 g/2 oz freshly grated
Parmesan cheese
salt and freshly ground
black pepper

To serve:

cherry tomatoes
fresh green salad leaves

Bring a large pan of lightly salted water to a rolling boil. Add the rigatoni and cook according to the packet instructions, or until *al dente*. Drain the pasta thoroughly, reserve and keep warm.

Melt the butter in a large saucepan or wok over a medium heat. Add the Gorgonzola cheese and stir until just melted. Add the brandy if using and cook for 30 seconds, then pour in the cream and cook for 1–2 minutes, stirring until the sauce is smooth.

Stir in the walnut pieces, basil and half the Parmesan cheese, then add the rigatoni. Season to taste with salt and pepper. Return to the heat, stirring frequently, until heated through. Divide the pasta among four warmed pasta bowls, sprinkle with the remaining Parmesan cheese and serve immediately with cherry tomatoes and fresh green salad leaves.

Pumpkin-filled Pasta with Butter & Sage

Serves 6–8

1 quantity fresh pasta dough,
see page 4
125 g/4 oz butter
2 tbsp freshly shredded sage leaves
50 g/2 oz freshly grated Parmesan
cheese, to serve

For the filling:

250 g/9 oz freshly cooked pumpkin
or sweet potato flesh, mashed
and cooled
75–125 g/3–4 oz dried breadcrumbs
125 g/4 oz freshly grated
Parmesan cheese
1 medium egg yolk
$1/2$ tsp soft brown sugar
2 tbsp freshly chopped parsley
freshly grated nutmeg
salt and freshly ground black pepper

Mix together the ingredients for the filling in a bowl, seasoning to taste with freshly grated nutmeg, salt and pepper. If the mixture seems too wet, add a few more breadcrumbs to bind.

Cut the pasta dough into quarters. Work with one at a time, covering the remaining quarters with a damp tea towel. Roll out a quarter very thinly into a strip 10 cm/4 inches wide. Drop spoonfuls of the filling along the strip 6.5 cm/2$1/2$ inches apart, in 2 rows about 5 cm/2 inches apart. Moisten the outside edges and the spaces between the filling with water.

Roll out another strip of pasta and lay it over the filled strip. Press down gently along both edges and between the filled sections. Using a fluted pastry wheel, cut along both long sides, down the centre and between the fillings to form cushions. Transfer the cushions to a lightly floured baking sheet. Continue making cushions and allow to dry for 30 minutes.

Bring a large saucepan of slightly salted water to the boil. Add the pasta cushions and return to the boil. Cook, stirring frequently, for 4–5 minutes, or until *al dente*. Drain carefully.

Heat the butter in a pan, stir in the shredded sage leaves and cook for 30 seconds. Add the pasta cushions, stir gently then spoon into serving bowls. Sprinkle with the grated Parmesan cheese and serve immediately.

Singapore Noodles

Serves 4

225 g/8 oz thin round egg noodles
3 tbsp groundnut or vegetable oil
125 g/4 oz field mushrooms, wiped
and thinly sliced
2.5 cm/1 inch piece root ginger,
peeled and finely chopped
1 red chilli, deseeded and thinly sliced
1 red pepper, deseeded and
thinly sliced
2 garlic cloves, peeled and crushed
1 medium courgette, cut in half
lengthwise and diagonally sliced
4–6 spring onions, trimmed and
thinly sliced
50 g/2 oz frozen garden peas, thawed
1 tbsp curry paste
2 tbsp tomato ketchup
salt or soy sauce
125 g/4 oz beansprouts, rinsed
and drained
sesame seeds and fresh coriander
leaves, to garnish

Bring a large pan of lightly salted water to a rolling boil. Add the noodles and cook according to the packet instructions, or until *al dente*. Drain thoroughly and toss with 1 tablespoon of the oil.

Heat the remaining oil in a wok or large frying pan over high heat. Add the mushrooms, ginger, chilli and red pepper and stir-fry for 2 minutes. Add the garlic, courgettes, spring onions and garden peas to the pan and stir lightly.

Push the vegetables to one side and add the curry paste, tomato ketchup and about 125 ml/4 fl oz hot water. Season to taste with salt or a few drops of soy sauce and allow to boil vigorously, stirring, until the paste is smooth.

Stir the reserved egg noodles and the beansprouts into the vegetable mixture and stir-fry until coated with the paste and thoroughly heated through. Season with more soy sauce if necessary, then turn into a large warmed serving bowl or spoon on to individual plates. Garnish with sesame seeds and coriander leaves. Serve immediately.

Tortellini, Cherry Tomato Mozzarella Skewers

Serves 6

250 g/9 oz mixed green and plain
cheese or vegetable-filled
fresh tortellini
150 ml/ ¹/₄ pint extra virgin olive oil
2 garlic cloves, peeled and crushed
pinch dried thyme or basil
salt and freshly ground
black pepper
225 g/8 oz cherry tomatoes
450 g/1 lb mozzarella, cut into
2.5 cm/1 inch cubes
basil leaves, to garnish
dressed salad leaves, to serve

Preheat the grill and line a grill pan with tinfoil, just before cooking. Bring a large pan of lightly salted water to a rolling boil. Add the tortellini and cook according to the packet instructions, or until *al dente*. Drain, rinse under cold running water, drain again and toss with 2 tablespoons of the olive oil and reserve.

Pour the remaining olive oil into a small bowl. Add the crushed garlic and thyme or basil, then blend well. Season to taste with salt and black pepper and reserve.

To assemble the skewers, thread the tortellini alternately with the cherry tomatoes and cubes of mozzarella. Arrange the skewers on the grill pan and brush generously on all sides with the olive oil mixture.

Cook the skewers under the preheated grill for about 5 minutes, or until they begin to turn golden, turning them halfway through cooking. Arrange 2 skewers on each plate and garnish with a few basil leaves. Serve immediately with dressed salad leaves.

Tortellini & Summer Vegetable Salad

Serves 6

350 g/12 oz mixed green and plain
cheese-filled fresh tortellini
150 ml/ ¼ pint extra virgin olive oil
225 g/8 oz fine green
beans, trimmed
175 g/6 oz broccoli florets
1 yellow or red pepper, deseeded
and thinly sliced
1 red onion, peeled and sliced
175 g jar marinated artichoke hearts,
drained and halved
2 tbsp capers
75 g/3 oz dry-cured pitted
black olives
3 tbsp raspberry or balsamic vinegar
1 tbsp Dijon mustard
1 tsp soft brown sugar
salt and freshly ground black pepper
2 tbsp freshly chopped basil or flat
leaf parsley
2 quartered hard-boiled eggs,
to garnish

Bring a large pan of lightly salted water to a rolling boil. Add the tortellini and cook according to the packet instructions, or until *al dente*.

Using a large slotted spoon, transfer the tortellini to a colander to drain. Rinse under cold running water and drain again. Transfer to a large bowl and toss with 2 tablespoons of the olive oil.

Return the pasta water to the boil and drop in the green beans and broccoli florets; blanch them for 2 minutes, or until just beginning to soften. Drain, rinse under cold running water and drain again thoroughly. Add the vegetables to the reserved tortellini.

Add the pepper, onion, artichoke hearts, capers and olives to the bowl; stir lightly.

Whisk together the vinegar, mustard and brown sugar in a bowl and season to taste with salt and pepper. Slowly whisk in the remaining olive oil to form a thick, creamy dressing. Pour over the tortellini and vegetables, add the chopped basil or parsley and stir until lightly coated. Transfer to a shallow serving dish or salad bowl. Garnish with the hard-boiled egg quarters and serve.

Ententertaining

Although many people consider pasta as the basis for only a simple everyday meal, it can in fact make the ideal showstopping dish for a special occasion or dinner party. Guests will certainly be impressed by the flavoursome Salmon & Mushroom Linguine, whilst the luxurious Farfalle & Chicken in White Wine Sauce will leave them asking for second helpings!

Fettuccine with Calves' Liver & Calvados

Serves 4

450 g/1 lb calves' liver, trimmed
and thinly sliced
50 g/2 oz plain flour
salt and freshly ground
black pepper
1 tsp paprika
50 g/2 oz butter
1½ tbsp olive oil
2 tbsp Calvados
150 ml/ ¼ pint cider
150 ml/ ¼ pint whipping cream
350 g/12 oz fresh fettuccine
fresh thyme sprigs, to garnish

Season the flour with the salt, black pepper and paprika, then toss the liver in the flour until well coated.

Melt half the butter and 1 tablespoon of the olive oil in a large frying pan and fry the liver in batches for 1 minute, or until just browned but still slightly pink inside. Remove using a slotted spoon and place in a warmed dish.

Add the remaining butter to the pan, stir in 1 tablespoon of the seasoned flour and cook for 1 minute. Pour in the Calvados and cider and cook over a high heat for 30 seconds. Stir the cream into the sauce and simmer for 1 minute to thicken slightly, then season to taste. Return the liver to the pan and heat through.

Bring a large pan of lightly salted water to a rolling boil. Add the fettuccine and cook according to the packet instructions, about 3–4 minutes, or until *al dente*.

Drain the fettuccine thoroughly, return to the pan and toss in the remaining oil. Divide among four plates and spoon the liver and sauce over the pasta. Garnish with thyme sprigs and serve immediately.

Tagliatelle with Stuffed Pork Escalopes

Serves 4

150 g/5 oz broccoli florets, finely
chopped and blanched
125 g/4 oz mozzarella
cheese, grated
1 garlic clove, peeled and crushed
2 large eggs, beaten
salt and freshly ground
black pepper
4 thin pork escalopes, weighing
about 100 g/3^1/$_2$ oz each
1 tbsp olive oil
25 g/1 oz butter
2 tbsp flour
150 ml/ ^{1}/$_4$ pint milk
150 ml/ ^{1}/$_4$ pint chicken stock
1 tbsp Dijon mustard
225 g/8 oz fresh tagliatelle
sage leaves, to garnish

Preheat the oven to 180°C/350°F/Gas Mark 4, 10 minutes before cooking. Mix the broccoli with the mozzarella cheese, garlic and beaten eggs. Season to taste with salt and pepper and reserve.

Using a meat mallet or rolling pin, pound the escalopes on a sheet of greaseproof paper until 5 mm/¼ inch thick. Divide the broccoli mixture between the escalopes and roll each one up from the shortest side. Place the pork rolls in a lightly oiled ovenproof dish, drizzle over the olive oil and bake in the preheated oven for 40–50 minutes, or until cooked.

Meanwhile, melt the butter in a heavy-based pan, stir in the flour and cook for 2 minutes. Remove from the heat and whisk in the milk and stock. Season to taste, stir in the mustard then cook until smooth and thickened. Keep warm.

Bring a large pan of lightly salted water to a rolling boil. Add the taglietelle and cook according to the packet instructions, about 3–4 minutes, or until *al dente*. Drain thoroughly and tip into a warmed serving dish. Slice each pork roll into three, place on top of the pasta and pour the sauce over. Garnish with sage leaves and serve immediately.

Spicy Chicken with Open Ravioli & Tomato Sauce

Serves 2–3

2 tbsp olive oil
1 onion, peeled and finely chopped
1 tsp ground cumin
1 tsp hot paprika pepper
1 tsp ground cinnamon
175 g/6 oz boneless and skinless
chicken breasts, chopped
salt and freshly ground
black pepper
1 tbsp smooth peanut butter
50 g/2 oz butter
1 shallot, peeled and finely chopped
2 garlic cloves, peeled and crushed
400 g can chopped tomatoes
125 g/4 oz fresh egg lasagne
2 tbsp freshly chopped coriander

Heat the olive oil in a frying pan, add the onion and cook gently for 2–3 minutes then add the cumin, paprika pepper and cinnamon and cook for a further 1 minute. Add the chicken, season to taste with salt and pepper and cook for 3–4 minutes, or until tender. Add the peanut butter and stir until well mixed and reserve.

Melt the butter in the frying pan, add the shallot and cook for 2 minutes. Add the tomatoes and garlic and season to taste. Simmer gently for 20 minutes, or until thickened, then keep the sauce warm.

Cut each sheet of lasagne into six squares. Bring a large pan of lightly salted water to a rolling boil. Add the lasagne squares and cook according to the packet instructions, about 3–4 minutes, or until *al dente*. Drain the lasagne pieces thoroughly, reserve and keep warm.

Layer the pasta squares with the spicy filling on individual warmed plates. Pour over a little of the hot tomato sauce and sprinkle with chopped coriander. Serve immediately.

Farfalle & Chicken in White Wine Sauce

Serves 4

4 boneless and skinless chicken
breasts, about 450 g/1 lb in
total weight
salt and freshly ground
black pepper
125 g/4 oz feta cheese
1 small egg, beaten
2 tbsp freshly chopped tarragon
50 g/2 oz butter
1 tbsp olive oil
1 onion, peeled and sliced
into rings
150 ml/¹/₄ pint white wine
150 ml/¹/₄ pint chicken stock
350 g/12 oz fresh farfalle
3–4 tbsp soured cream
2 tbsp freshly chopped parsley

Place the chicken breasts between two sheets of greaseproof paper and, using a meat mallet or wooden rolling pin, pound as thinly as possible. Season with salt and pepper and reserve.

Mash the feta cheese with a fork and blend with the egg and half the tarragon. Divide the mixture between the chicken breasts and roll up each one. Secure with cocktail sticks.

Heat half the butter and all the olive oil in a frying pan, add the onion and cook for 2–3 minutes. Remove, using a slotted spoon, and reserve. Add the chicken parcels to the pan and cook for 3–4 minutes, or until browned. Pour in the wine and the stock and stir in the remaining tarragon. Cover and simmer gently for 10–15 minutes, or until the chicken is cooked.

Meanwhile, bring a large pan of lightly salted water to a rolling boil. Add the farfalle and cook according to the packet instructions, about 3–4 minutes, or until *al dente*. Drain, toss in the remaining butter and tip into a warmed serving dish.

Slice each chicken roll into four and place on the pasta. Whisk the sauce until smooth, then stir in the soured cream and the reserved onions. Heat the sauce gently, then pour over the chicken. Sprinkle with the parsley and serve immediately.

Gnocchi Roulade with Mozzarella & Spinach

Serves 8

600 ml/1 pint milk
125 g/4 oz fine semolina or polenta
25 g/1 oz butter
75 g/3 oz Cheddar cheese, grated
2 medium egg yolks
salt and freshly ground
black pepper
700 g/1½ lb baby spinach leaves
½ tsp freshly grated nutmeg
1 garlic clove, peeled and crushed
2 tbsp olive oil
150 g/5 oz mozzarella
cheese, grated
2 tbsp freshly grated
Parmesan cheese
freshly made tomato sauce,
to serve

Preheat the oven to 240°C/475°F/Gas Mark 9, 15 minutes before cooking. Oil and line a large Swiss roll tin (23 cm/9 inch x 33 cm/13 inch) with non-stick baking parchment.

Pour the milk into a heavy-based pan and whisk in the semolina. Bring to the boil then simmer, stirring continuously with a wooden spoon, for 3–4 minutes, or until very thick. Remove from heat and stir in the butter and Cheddar cheese until melted. Whisk in the egg yolks and season to taste with salt and pepper. Pour into the lined tin. Cover and allow to cool for 1 hour.

Cook the baby spinach in batches in a large pan with 1 teaspoon of water for 3–4 minutes, or until wilted. Drain thoroughly, season to taste with salt, pepper and nutmeg, then allow to cool.

Spread the spinach over the cooled semolina mixture and sprinkle over 75 g/3 oz of the mozzarella and half the Parmesan cheese. Bake in the preheated oven for 20 minutes, or until golden.

Allow to cool, then roll up like a Swiss roll. Sprinkle with the remaining mozzarella and Parmesan cheese, then bake for another 15–20 minutes, or until golden. Serve immediately with freshly made tomato sauce.

Spaghetti with Smoked Salmon & Tiger Prawns

Serves 4

225 g/8 oz baby spinach leaves
salt and freshly ground
black pepper
pinch freshly grated nutmeg
225 g/8 oz cooked tiger prawns in
their shells, cooked
450 g/1 lb fresh angel hair
spaghetti
50 g/2 oz butter
3 medium eggs
1 tbsp freshly chopped dill, plus
extra to garnish
125 g/4 oz smoked salmon,
cut into strips
dill sprigs, to garnish
2 tbsp grated Parmesan cheese,
to serve

Cook the baby spinach leaves in a large pan with 1 teaspoon of water for 3–4 minutes, or until wilted. Drain thoroughly, season to taste with salt, pepper and nutmeg and keep warm. Remove the shells from all but four of the tiger prawns and reserve.

Bring a large pan of lightly salted water to a rolling boil. Add the pasta and cook according to the packet instructions, about 3–4 minutes, or until *al dente*. Drain thoroughly and return to the pan. Stir in the butter and the peeled prawns, cover and keep warm.

Beat the eggs with the dill, season well, then stir into the spaghetti and prawns. Return the pan to the heat briefly, just long enough to lightly scramble the eggs, then remove from the heat. Carefully mix in the smoked salmon strips and the cooked spinach. Toss gently to mix. Tip into a warmed serving dish and garnish with the reserved prawns and dill sprigs. Serve immediately with grated Parmesan cheese.

Pasta Ring with Chicken Sun-dried Tomatoes

Serves 6

125 g/4 oz butter, plus extra
for brushing
2 tbsp natural white breadcrumbs
40 g/1½ oz flour
450 ml/ ¾ pint milk
1 small onion, peeled and very
finely chopped
salt and freshly ground
black pepper
225 g/8 oz fresh tagliatelle
450 g/1 lb chicken breast fillets,
skinned and cut into strips
200 ml/7 fl oz white wine
1 tsp cornflour
2 tbsp freshly chopped tarragon
2 tbsp chopped sun-dried tomatoes

Preheat the oven to 190°C/375°F/Gas Mark 5, 10 minutes before cooking. Lightly brush a 20.5 cm/8 inch ring mould with a little melted butter and dust with the breadcrumbs.

Melt 50 g/2 oz of the butter in a heavy-based pan. Add the flour and cook for 1 minute. Whisk in the milk and cook, stirring, until thickened. Add the chopped onion, season to taste with salt and pepper and reserve.

Bring a large pan of lightly salted water to a rolling boil. Add the tagliatelle and cook according to the packet instructions, about 3–4 minutes, or until *al dente*. Drain thoroughly and stir into the white sauce. Pour the pasta mixture into the prepared mould and bake in the preheated oven for 25–30 minutes.

Melt the remaining butter in a frying pan, add the chicken and cook for 4–5 minutes, or until cooked. Pour in the wine and cook over a high heat for 30 seconds. Blend the cornflour with 1 teaspoon of water and stir into the pan. Add 1 tablespoon chopped tarragon and the tomatoes. Season well, then cook for a few minutes, until thickened.

Allow the pasta to cool for 5 minutes, then unmould on to a large serving plate. Fill the centre with the chicken sauce. Garnish with the remaining tarragon and serve immediately.

Salmon Mushroom Linguine

Serves 4

450 g/1 lb salmon fillets, skinned
salt and freshly ground
black pepper
75 g/3 oz butter
40 g/1 ¹/₂ oz flour
300 ml/ ¹/₂ pint chicken stock
150 ml/ ¹/₄ pint whipping cream
225 g/8 oz mushrooms, wiped
and sliced
350 g/12 oz linguine
50 g/2 oz Cheddar cheese, grated
50 g/2 oz fresh white breadcrumbs
2 tbsp freshly chopped parsley,
to garnish

Preheat the oven to 190°C/375°F/Gas Mark 5, 10 minutes before cooking. Place the salmon in a shallow pan and cover with water. Season well with salt and pepper and bring to the boil, then lower the heat and simmer for 6–8 minutes, or until cooked. Drain and keep warm.

Melt 50 g/2 oz of the butter in a heavy-based pan, stir in the flour, cook for 1 minute then whisk in the chicken stock. Simmer gently until thickened. Stir in the cream and season to taste. Keep the sauce warm.

Melt the remaining butter, in a pan, add the sliced mushrooms and cook for 2–3 minutes. Stir the mushrooms into the white sauce.

Bring a large pan of lightly salted water to a rolling boil. Add the linguine and cook according to the packet instructions, or until *al dente*.

Drain the pasta thoroughly and return to the pan. Stir in half the sauce, then spoon into a lightly oiled a 1.4 litre/2½ pint shallow ovenproof dish. Flake the salmon, add to the remaining sauce then pour over the pasta. Sprinkle with the cheese and breadcrumbs, then bake in the preheated for 15–20 minutes, or until golden. Garnish with the parsley and serve immediately.

Spaghetti with Hot Chilli Mussels

Serves 4

900 g/2 lb fresh live mussels
300 ml/ ½ pint white wine
3–4 garlic cloves, peeled
and crushed
2 tbsp olive oil
1–2 bird's-eye chillies, deseeded
and chopped
2 x 400 g cans chopped tomatoes
salt and freshly ground
black pepper
350 g/12 oz fresh spaghetti
2 tbsp freshly chopped parsley,
to garnish
warm crusty bread, to serve

Scrub the mussels and remove any beards. Discard any that do not close when tapped. Place in a large pan with the white wine and half the crushed garlic. Cover and cook over a high heat for 5–6 minutes, shaking the pan from time to time. When the mussels have opened, drain, reserving the juices and straining them through a muslin-lined sieve. Discard any mussels that have not opened and keep the rest warm.

Heat the olive oil in a heavy-based pan, add the remaining garlic with the chillies and cook for 30 seconds. Stir in the chopped tomatoes and 75 ml/3 fl oz of the reserved cooking liquor and simmer for 15–20 minutes. Season to taste with salt and pepper.

Meanwhile, bring a large pan of lightly salted water to a rolling boil. Add the spaghetti and cook according to the packet instructions, about 3–4 minutes, or until *al dente*.

Drain the spaghetti thoroughly and return to the pan. Add the mussels and tomato sauce to the pasta, toss lightly to cover, then tip into a warmed serving dish or spoon on to individual plates. Garnish with chopped parsley and serve immediately with warm crusty bread.

Conchiglioni with Crab au Gratin

Serves 4

175 g/6 oz large pasta shells
50 g/2 oz butter
1 shallot, peeled and finely chopped
1 bird's-eye chilli, deseeded and
finely chopped
2 x 200 g cans crabmeat, drained
3 tbsp plain flour
50 ml/2 fl oz white wine
50 ml/2 fl oz milk
3 tbsp crème fraîche
15 g/ ½ oz Cheddar cheese, grated
salt and freshly ground black pepper
1 tbsp oil or melted butter
50 g/2 oz fresh white breadcrumbs

To serve:

cheese or tomato sauce
tossed green salad or freshly cooked
baby vegetables

Preheat the oven to 200°C/400°F/Gas Mark 6, 15 minutes before cooking. Bring a large pan of lightly salted water to a rolling boil. Add the pasta shells and cook according to the packet instructions, or until *al dente*. Drain thoroughly and allow to dry completely.

Melt half the butter in a heavy-based pan, add the shallots and chilli and cook for 2 minutes, then stir in the crabmeat. Stuff the cooled shells with the crab mixture and reserve.

Melt the remaining butter in a small pan and stir in the flour. Cook for 1 minute, then whisk in the wine and milk and cook, stirring, until thickened. Stir in the crème fraîche and grated cheese and season the sauce to taste with salt and pepper.

Place the crab filled shells in a lightly oiled, large shallow baking dish or tray and spoon a little of the sauce over. Toss the breadcrumbs in the melted butter or oil, then sprinkle over the pasta shells. Bake in the preheated oven for 10 minutes. Serve immediately with a cheese or tomato sauce and a tossed green salad or cooked baby vegetables.

Pappardelle with Spicy Lamb & Peppers

Serves 4

450 g/1 lb fresh lamb mince
2 tbsp olive oil
1 onion, peeled and finely chopped
2 garlic cloves, peeled and crushed
1 green pepper, deseeded
and chopped
1 yellow pepper, deseeded
and chopped
$^1/_2$ tsp hot chilli powder
1 tsp ground cumin
1 tbsp tomato paste
150 ml/ $^1/_4$ pint red wine
salt and freshly ground black pepper
350 g/12 oz pappardelle
2 oz fresh white breadcrumbs
25 g/1 oz butter, melted
25 g/1 oz Cheddar cheese, grated
1 tbsp freshly chopped parsley

Preheat the grill just before cooking. Dry fry the minced lamb in a frying pan until browned. Heat the olive oil in a heavy-based pan, add the onion, garlic and all the chopped peppers and cook for 3–4 minutes, or until softened. Add the browned lamb mince to the pan and cook stirring, until the onions have softened, then drain off any remaining oil.

Stir the chilli powder and cumin into the pan and cook gently for 2 minutes, stirring frequently. Add the tomato paste, pour in the wine and season to taste with salt and pepper. Reduce the heat and simmer for 10–15 minutes, or until the sauce has reduced.

Meanwhile, bring a large pan of lightly salted water to a rolling boil. Add the pappardelle and cook according to the packet instructions, or until *al dente*. Drain thoroughly, then return to the pan and stir the meat sauce into the pasta. Keep warm.

Meanwhile, place the breadcrumbs on a baking tray, drizzle over the melted butter and place under the preheated grill for 3–4 minutes, or until golden and crispy. Allow to cool, then mix with the grated Cheddar cheese. Tip the pasta mixture into a warmed serving dish, sprinkle with the breadcrumbs and the parsley. Serve immediately.

Farfalle with Courgettes Mushrooms

Serves 4

25 g/1 oz butter
2 tsp olive oil
1 small onion, peeled and finely chopped
2 garlic cloves, peeled and crushed
125 g/4 oz bacon lardons
450 g/1 lb courgettes, trimmed and diced
125 g/4 oz button mushrooms, wiped and roughly chopped
350 g/12 oz farfalle
salt and freshly ground black pepper
250 ml carton crème fraîche
2 tbsp freshly chopped parsley
shaved pecorino cheese, to garnish

To serve:

mixed salad
crusty bread

Heat the butter and olive oil in a large pan, add the onion, garlic and bacon lardons and cook for 3–4 minutes, or until the onion has softened. Add the courgettes and cook, stirring, for a further 3–4 minutes. Add the mushrooms, lower the heat and cook, covered, for a further 4–5 minutes.

Meanwhile, bring a large pan of lightly salted water to a rolling boil. Add the fusilli and cook according to the packet instructions, or until *al dente*. Drain thoroughly, return to the pan and keep warm.

Season the mushroom mixture to taste with salt and pepper, then stir in the crème fraîche and half the chopped parsley. Simmer for 2–3 minutes, or until the sauce is thick and creamy.

Pour the sauce over the cooked pasta, toss lightly, then reheat for 2 minutes, or until piping hot. Tip into a warmed serving dish and sprinkle over the chopped parsley. Garnish with pecorino cheese shavings and serve immediately with a mixed salad and crusty bread.

Cannelloni with Tomato ﹩ Red Wine Sauce

Serves 6

2 tbsp olive oil
1 onion, peeled and finely chopped
1 garlic clove, peeled and crushed
250 g carton ricotta cheese
50 g/2 oz pine nuts
salt and freshly ground black pepper
pinch freshly grated nutmeg
250 g/9 oz fresh spinach lasagne
25 g/1 oz butter
1 shallot, peeled and finely chopped
150 ml/ ^{1}/$_4$ pint red wine
400 g can chopped tomatoes
^{1}/$_2$ tsp sugar
50 g/2 oz mozzarella cheese, grated,
plus extra to serve
1 tbsp freshly chopped parsley,
to garnish
fresh green salad, to serve

Preheat the oven to 200°C/400°F/Gas Mark 6, 15 minutes before cooking. Heat the oil in a heavy-based pan, add the onion and garlic and cook for 2–3 minutes. Cool slightly, then stir in the ricotta cheese and pine nuts. Season the filling to taste with salt, pepper and the nutmeg.

Cut each lasagne sheet in half, put a little of the ricotta filling on each piece and roll up like a cigar to resemble cannelloni tubes. Arrange the cannelloni, seam-side down, in a single layer, in a lightly oiled, 2.3 litre/ 4 pint shallow ovenproof dish.

Melt the butter in a pan, add the shallot and cook for 2 minutes. Pour in the red wine, tomatoes and sugar and season well. Bring to the boil, lower the heat and simmer for about 20 minutes, or until thickened. Add a little more sugar if desired. Transfer to a food processor and blend until a smooth sauce is formed.

Pour the warm tomato sauce over the cannelloni and sprinkle with the grated mozzarella cheese. Bake in the preheated oven for about 30 minutes, or until golden-brown and bubbling. Garnish and serve immediately with a green salad.

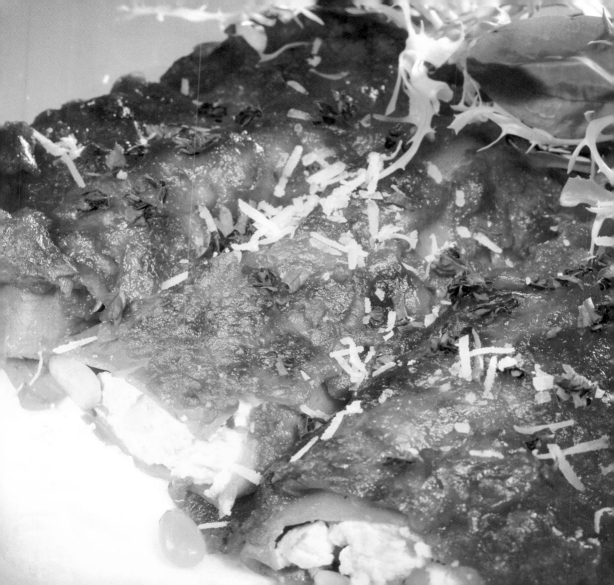

Aubergine Tomato Layer

Serves 4

2 aubergines, about 700 g/1¹/₂ lb,
trimmed and thinly sliced
6 tbsp olive oil
1 onion, peeled and finely sliced
1 garlic clove, peeled and crushed
400 g can chopped tomatoes
50 ml/2 fl oz red wine
¹/₂ tsp sugar
salt and freshly ground
black pepper
50 g/2 oz butter
40 g/1¹/₂ oz flour
450 ml/ ³/₄ pint milk
225 g/8 oz fresh egg lasagne
2 medium eggs, beaten
200 ml/7 fl oz Greek yogurt
125 g/3 oz mozzarella
cheese, grated
fresh basil leaves, to garnish

Preheat the oven to 190°C/375°F/Gas Mark 5, 10 minutes before cooking. Brush the aubergine slices with 5 tablespoons of the olive oil and place on a baking sheet. Bake in the preheated oven for 20 minutes, or until tender. Remove from the oven and increase the temperature to 200°C/400°F/Gas Mark 6.

Heat the remaining oil in a heavy-based pan. Add the onion and garlic, cook for 2–3 minutes then add the tomatoes, wine and sugar. Season to taste with salt and pepper, then simmer for 20 minutes.

Melt the butter in another pan. Stir in the flour, cook for 2 minutes, then whisk in the milk. Cook for 2–3 minutes, or until thickened. Season to taste.

Pour a little white sauce into a lightly oiled, 1.7 litre/3 pint baking dish. Cover with a layer of lasagne, spread with tomato sauce, then add some of the aubergines. Cover thinly with white sauce and sprinkle with a little cheese. Continue to layer in this way, finishing with a layer of lasagne.

Beat together the eggs and yogurt. Season, then pour over the lasagne. Sprinkle with the remaining cheese and bake in the preheated oven for 25–30 minutes, or until golden. Garnish with basil leaves and serve.

Cannelloni with Gorgonzola Sauce

Serves 2–3

50 g/2 oz salted butter
1 shallot, peeled and finely chopped
2 rashers streaky bacon, rind removed and chopped
225 g/8 oz mushrooms, wiped and finely chopped
25 g/1 oz plain flour
120 ml/4 fl oz double cream
125 g/4 oz fresh egg lasagne, 6 sheets in total
40 g/1¹/₂ oz unsalted butter
150 g/5 oz Gorgonzola cheese, diced
150 ml/ ¹/₄ pint whipping cream
assorted salad leaves, to serve

Preheat the oven to 190°C/375°F/Gas Mark 5, 10 minutes before cooking. Melt the salted butter in a heavy-based pan, add the shallot and bacon and cook for about 4–5 minutes.

Add the mushrooms to the pan and cook for 5–6 minutes, or until the mushrooms are very soft. Stir in the flour, cook for 1 minute, then stir in the double cream and cook gently for 2 minutes. Allow to cool.

Cut each sheet of lasagne in half. Spoon some filling on to each piece and roll up from the longest side to resemble cannelloni. Arrange the cannelloni in a lightly oiled, shallow 1.4 litre/2¹/₂ pint ovenproof dish.

Heat the unsalted butter very slowly in a pan and when melted, add the Gorgonzola cheese. Stir until the cheese has melted, then stir in the whipping cream. Bring to the boil slowly, then simmer gently for about 5 minutes, or until thickened.

Pour the cream sauce over the cannelloni. Place in the preheated oven and bake for 20 minutes, or until golden and thoroughly heated through. Serve immediately with assorted salad leaves.

Ratatouille Pasta Bake

Serves 4

1 tbsp olive oil
2 large onions, peeled and
finely chopped
400 g can chopped tomatoes
100 ml/3¹/₂ fl oz white wine
¹/₂ tsp caster sugar
salt and freshly ground black pepper
40 g/1¹/₂ oz butter
2 garlic cloves, peeled and crushed
125 g/4 oz mushrooms, wiped and
thickly sliced
700 g/1¹/₂ lb courgettes, trimmed
and thickly sliced
125 g/4 oz fresh spinach lasagne
2 large eggs
2 tbsp double cream
75 g/3 oz mozzarella cheese, grated
25 g/1 oz pecorino cheese, grated
green salad, to serve

Preheat the oven to 190°C/375°F/Gas Mark 5, 10 minutes before cooking. Heat the olive oil in a heavy-based pan, add half the onion and cook gently for 2–3 minutes. Stir in the tomatoes and wine, then simmer for 20 minutes, or until a thick consistency is formed. Add the sugar and season to taste with salt and pepper. Reserve.

Meanwhile, melt the butter in another pan, add the remaining onion, the garlic, mushrooms and courgettes and cook gently for 10 minutes, or until softened.

Spread a little tomato sauce in the base of a lightly oiled, 1.4 litre/ 2¹/₂ pint baking dish. Top with a layer of lasagne and spoon over half the mushroom and courgette mixture. Repeat the layers, finishing with a layer of lasagne.

Beat the eggs and cream together, then pour over the lasagne. Mix the mozzarella and pecorino cheeses together then sprinkle on top of the lasagne. Place in the preheated oven and cook for 20 minutes, or until golden-brown. Serve immediately with a green salad.

Lamb Pasta Pie

Serves 8

400 g/14 oz plain white flour
100 g/3½ oz margarine
100 g/3½ oz white vegetable fat
pinch of salt
1 small egg, separated
50 g/2 oz butter
50 g/2 oz flour
450 ml/ ¾ pint milk
salt and freshly ground
black pepper
225 g/8 oz macaroni
50 g/2 oz Cheddar cheese, grated
1 tbsp vegetable oil
1 onion, peeled and chopped
1 garlic clove, peeled
and crushed
2 celery sticks, trimmed
and chopped
450 g/1 lb lamb mince
1 tbsp tomato paste
400 g can chopped tomatoes

Preheat the oven to 190°C/375°F/Gas Mark 5, 10 minutes before cooking. Lightly oil a 20.5 cm/8 inch spring-form cake tin. Blend the flour, salt, margarine and white vegetable fat in a food processor and add sufficient cold water to make a smooth, pliable dough. Knead on a lightly floured surface, then roll out two-thirds to line the base and sides of the tin. Brush the pastry with egg white and reserve.

Melt the butter in a heavy-based pan, stir in the flour and cook gently for 2 minutes. Stir in the milk and cook, stirring, until a smooth, thick sauce is formed. Season to taste with salt and pepper and reserve.

Bring a large pan of lightly salted water to a rolling boil. Add the macaroni and cook according to the packet instructions, or until *al dente*. Drain, then stir into the white sauce with the grated cheese.

Heat the oil in a pan, add the onion, garlic, celery and mince and cook, stirring, for 5–6 minutes. Stir in the tomato paste and tomatoes and cook for 10 minutes. Cool slightly. Place half the pasta mixture, then all the mince in the pastry-lined tin. Top with a layer of pasta. Roll out the remaining pastry and cut out a lid. Brush the edge with water, place over the filling and pinch the edges together. Use trimmings to decorate the top. Brush with beaten yolk and bake for 50–60 minutes, covering with foil if browning too quickly. Stand for 15 minutes before turning out. Serve immediately.

Baked Macaroni with Mushrooms & Leeks

Serves 4

2 tbsp olive oil
1 onion, peeled and finely chopped
1 garlic clove, peeled and crushed
2 small leeks, trimmed and chopped
450 g/1 lb assorted wild
mushrooms, trimmed
50 ml/2 fl oz white wine
75 g/3 oz butter
150 ml/ 1/4 pint crème fraîche or
whipping cream
salt and freshly ground black pepper
75 g/3 oz fresh white breadcrumbs
350 g/12 oz short cut macaroni
1 tbsp freshly chopped parsley,
to garnish

Preheat the oven to 220°C/425°F/Gas Mark 7, 15 minutes before cooking. Heat 1 tablespoon of the olive oil in a large frying pan, add the onion and garlic and cook for 2 minutes. Add the leeks, mushrooms and 25 g/1 oz of the butter then cook for 5 minutes. Pour in the white wine, cook for 2 minutes then stir in the crème fraîche or cream. Season to taste with salt and pepper.

Meanwhile, bring a large pan of lightly salted water to the boil. Add the macaroni and cook according to the packet instructions, or until *al dente*.

Melt 25 g/1 oz of the butter with the remaining oil in a small frying pan. Add the breadcrumbs and fry until just beginning to turn golden-brown. Drain on absorbent kitchen paper.

Drain the pasta thoroughly, toss in the remaining butter then tip into a lightly oiled, 1.4 litre/2 1/2 pint shallow baking dish. Cover the pasta with the leek and mushroom mixture then sprinkle with the fried breadcrumbs. Bake in the preheated oven for 5–10 minutes, or until golden and crisp. Garnish with chopped parsley and serve.

Index

Index